Famous First
Bubbles

Famous First Bubbles

The Fundamentals of Early Manias

Peter M. Garber

The MIT Press
Cambridge, Massachusetts
London, England

First MIT Press paperback edition, 2001

©2000 Massachusetts Institute of Technology

This book was set by Best-set Typesetter Ltd., Hong Kong.

Printed and bound in the United States of America.

Library of Congress Cataloging-in-Publication Data

Garber, Peter M.
    Famous first bubbles: the fundamentals of early manias /
Peter M. Garber.
        p.   cm.
    Includes bibliographical references (p.) and index.
    ISBN 0-262-07204-1 (hc : alk. paper), 0-262-57153-6 (pb)
    1. Speculation—History.   2. Tulip mania, 17th century.
3. Law, John, 1671–1729.   4. Compagnie des Indes—History.
5. South Sea Bubble, Great Britain, 1720.   I. Title.
HG6005.G37   2000
332.63'228—dc21
                                                    00-027297

Contents

Preface

Bubbles lie at the intersection between finance, economics, and psychology. Recent explanations of large-scale asset price movements have leaned toward placing psychology first in the list, not only for episodes from the dim past but also for most events in the crisis years of 1997, 1998, and 1999. The evidence that will be developed in this book, however, indicates that the early bubbles at least were driven by fundamentals. They stem from the more basic intersection of finance and economics, with psychology at most in the background.

This book is about the three most famous bubbles—the Dutch tulipmania, the Mississippi Bubble, and the South Sea Bubble—all of which have served as examples of private capital markets gone haywire. On the contrary,

• The high prices of rare bulbs in the tulipmania—emphasized in most stories as the prima facie evidence for its madness—is a standard feature of markets in newly developed varieties, as is a rapid price decline.

- Even now, rare bulb varieties can carry a price equal in value to a substantial house.

- Little economic distress was associated with the end of the tulipmania.

- The stories that we have now stem mainly from a single source resulting from a moralistic campaign of the Dutch government.

- The speculation in common bulbs was a phenomenon lasting one month in the dreary Dutch winter of 1637. A drinking phenomenon held in the taverns, it occurred in the midst of a massive outbreak of bubonic plague and had no real consequence.

- The Mississippi Bubble was a large-scale money printing operation and a government debt-for-equity swap.

- The South Sea Bubble was also a debt-for-equity swap, although less well-grounded.

- Both bubbles were grandiose macroeconomic schemes launched or aided by high government officials and supported by the entire apparatus of the governments of England and France.

- Nevertheless, they are now interpreted as prime examples of the madness possible in *private* financial markets and of the need for government control and regulation.

Acknowledgments

This book results from my research on the early bubbles undertaken over the years. As its basis, it combines two papers, "Tulipmania" (*Journal of Political Economy*, 1989) and "Famous First Bubbles"(*Journal of Economic Perspectives*, 1990), and a conference volume chapter, "Who Put the Mania in the Tulipmania?" (in E. White, ed., *Crashes and Panics: The Lessons From History,* Homewood: Dow-Jones Irwin, 1990). I am grateful to Robert Flood, Herschel Grossman, Robert Hodrick, Salih Neftci, Stuart Parkinson, David Ribar, Rudiger Dornbusch, and James Peck for useful discussions, to Guido Imbens for resourceful research assistance, and to Marina van Dongen and Klaas Baks for helpful translations. Librarians at Harvard's Houghton, Kress, Arnold Arboretum, and Grey Herbarium Libraries and at the Massachusetts Horticultural Society provided valuable guidance. The late George Stigler at the *Journal of Political Economy* provided extensive editorial comment in developing the basic paper on tulipmania on which this book is based, and Joseph Stiglitz and Timothy Taylor at the *Journal of Economic Perspectives* as well as several anonymous referees both for journal review and for this book also contributed helpful suggestions. I have benefited from the comments of participants in workshops at Brown University, the Board of Governors of the Federal Reserve, CUNY, Columbia University, Queens University, UCLA, MIT, the IMF, and Northwestern.

I

The Bubble Interpretation

The Dutch tulipmania, the Mississippi Bubble, the South Sea Bubble—these are always invoked with every outbreak of great financial instability. So implanted are they in our literature, that they are now used more as synonyms for financial instability than as references to the particular events themselves. Along with words such as *herding* and the newly popular *irrational exuberance*, they now dominate the policymaking, academic rhetoric, and market commentary on all the recent crises.

In general, these events are viewed as outbursts of irrationality: self-generating surges of optimism that pump up asset prices and misallocate investments and resources to such a great extent that a crash and major financial and economic distress inevitably follow. Only some bizarre self-delusion or blindness could have prevented a participant from seeing the obvious, so these episodes are called forth almost as a form of ridicule for such losers.

This book presents the fundamental history of the three famous bubbles. But it is necessary first to come to grips with the meaning of the class of words spawned by them to understand how these events from so long ago serve the modern regulatory rhetoric. In this small introductory glossary—and I hope not too excessive a detour—I will first work through the meaning of these words and critique them. Then I will present and discuss the definition of the word *bubble* that can be found in the authoritative literature on the subject. Finally, I will return to the important role as rhetorical weapons played by the three most famous bubbles by looking at how even the *Financial Times* employed them to interpret the events of October 1998.

The Meanings of a Few Words

Bubbles

The classic word for these phenomena is *bubble*. Bubble is one of the most beautiful concepts in economics and finance in that it is a fuzzy word filled with import but lacking a solid operational definition. Thus, one can make whatever one wants of it. The definition of *bubble* most often used in economic research is that part of asset price movement that is unexplainable based on what we call fundamentals. Fundamentals are a collection of variables that we believe should drive asset prices. In the context of a particular model of asset price determination, if we have a serious misforecast of asset prices we might then say that there is a bubble.

This is no more than saying that there is something happening that we cannot explain, which we normally call a random disturbance. In asset pricing studies, we give it a name—*bubble*—and appeal to unverifiable psychological stories.

Psychological state of mind is not a measurable concept, especially years after an event. It does, however, provide a convenient way of explaining some phenomena in the market that cannot otherwise be explained.

Our existing or favorite models of fundamentals often cannot explain important observed phenomena in asset markets. We know that market psychology or *market sentiment* can be important, so we blame the inadequacy of our fundamental model vis-à-vis actual outcomes on unmeasurable market psychology.

Herding

Although used frequently these days to explain large capital flows, *herding* is a vague word, projecting the feeling that speculators are cattle, some kind of prey. The rigged image here is that investors go grazing passively from one place to another, following a leader, without scouting out the grass themselves. In particular, the herding concept has arisen recently in the context of large amounts of funds flowing into emerging markets.

Of course, herding is not an irrational act. If it is known that someone is good at analysis and that person makes a move, it is reasonable to follow. The problem is that those who call on herding as an explanation for the movement of funds by a large number of institutions or individuals into a particular market never provide any evidence of on what basis investors are making decisions. That we see large amounts of funds flowing in together at one time and flowing out together at another does not mean that herding is going on—that is, that one or two smart people are doing the analysis and that everyone is following blindly. Everyone may be doing analysis.

Alternatively, fund managers may delegate the serious research and analytical effort to a trusted research organization, which in turn advises many clients. That the individual fund manager does not have a research department does not mean he is acting blindly.

The future is always shrouded in fog: we never know what is coming, and yet we have to allocate investment resources according to our best guess at the future. To fill the gap, we have theories. Once in a while, a convincing theory emerges that allows us to visualize the future "better" than before. That is what economic research is about: generating concepts that we can use to interpret observed phenomena and perhaps to forecast phenomena. Every once in a while, a theory becomes dominant and perhaps convincing. Keynesianism was a convincing theory once, and governments *herded* on the basis of Keynesian policy prescriptions. These tended to fail in their more overblown forms, after which governments shied away from such policies and imposed (*herded* around) stringent anti-inflationist policies. No one says, though, that we observed herding behavior on the part of governments during the 1960s and 1970s when they bought into Keynesianism and during the 1980s and 1990s when they got out en masse.

Irrational Exuberance

This is a term recently invoked by Alan Greenspan, chairman of the Board of Governors of the Federal Reserve. It was simply part of a claim, as of December 1996 when the Dow was at about 6500, that the stock markets might be getting it wrong and that he might know better what the right level of stock prices should be (i.e., he gave a new name to the divergence of market prices from a theory of where they should be). He concluded that there might be irrationality afoot.

Three years later, with the stock market fifty percent higher, in testimony on February 23, 1999, Mr. Greenspan was asked whether he thought there was still irrational exuberance. His reply was "That is something you can only know after the fact." Thus, by denying its ability to predict, he removed all meaningful content from the concept.

Two Other Definitions of Bubble

To place a final emphasis on how tenuous and unusable the meaning of bubbles can be, let us focus on a pair of definitions of *bubble* that can be found at various stages in the economics literature.

The premodern definition of a bubble is from Palgrave's *Dictionary of Political Economy* (1926): "Any unsound undertaking accompanied by a high degree of speculation." This is basically the *irrational exuberance* definition of a bubble. By this definition, we cannot know if we have a bubble until after it bursts. Commercial undertakings accompanied by a high degree of speculation may actually turn out to be quite successful. It is only after we find out that a commercial undertaking did not work that we can conclude it was unsound and then call it a bubble. This concept is as empty as Greenspan's.

It is always possible that a scheme might succeed—if it does, it would then be described as brilliantly audacious. With the future often very uncertain, the only way that we can operate according to a purposeful plan is to postulate theories that allow us to forecast the future, given the current state of the world. These theories may be based on past experience but perhaps also on new phenomena that we observe.

If the theory is convincing, it will attract commercial and speculative activity. To return to the herding concept, speculators really gather around theories, not each other. If someone enters with a convincing story and structure of thought for organizing otherwise confusing phenomena, he will attract speculative capital. For instance, we know that the Internet stocks are a gamble, but they are backed by a theory of an epochal change in technology that will alter the entire economic structure. Normally careful governments are pushing this view to the extent that high officials even claim to have invented the Internet.

When there is a large technological shift, great uncertainty exists about what the future will bring. We do not know how the economic system will absorb all these changes, so naturally investment in many commercial undertakings suddenly becomes speculative, even in the old established businesses that may suffer if the theory comes true. These are almost required gambles on the future. If there is a convincing theory about the New Economy, we have to bet on it. We must allocate part of our portfolio to it. Otherwise, we might miss out on the next big winner or, even worse, be backing a loser. Therefore, we truly cannot know if the speculation was unsound until after the fact.

In his popular book on manias and bubbles, Kindleberger's definition of a *bubble* is as follows: "A bubble is an upward price movement over an extended range that then implodes." This is an empirical statement about the pattern of asset prices. A sort of chartist view of bubbles, this prescribes that we simply give a name to that particular price pattern. Such patterns can be observed in the data, so according to this definition, we cannot deny that a particular historical episode—for example, tulipmania or Mississippi Bubble—was a bubble. However, with this definition, there can be no necessary conclusion that this pattern reflects any irrationality or excess or was not based a priori on fundamentals, the usual reason for calling an event a bubble.

How These Bubbles Are Used to Sway Opinion

The concept of a bubble is a fuzzy one, which is why the concept itself can be debated incessantly. To short-circuit this poor definition, anyone aiming to explain current market phenomena in terms of bubbles is likely to cite the most famous historical examples—that is, to list phenomena such as the Dutch tulipmania, the Mississippi

Bubble, and the South Sea Bubble that everyone agrees
were outbursts of irrationality. By analogy, it is easier to
claim that there must be irrationality in the current
episodes.

As an example of how these famous bubbles are
always cited in periods of market stress, we can refer to
the lead editorial of the *Financial Times*, usually the most
careful of the financial press, which reviewed the IMF's
World Economic Outlook/Capital Markets Interim Report of
December 1998:

· "When everyone rushes in the same direction, it is hard
for financial speculators to stand aside and recall the
lessons of past stampedes."

· "Stories of the Dutch tulipmania in 1636 or the South
Sea Bubble eighty-four years later might have left deriv-
atives traders cold this summer; but the Mexico crisis
of 1994–1995 certainly should have created a warning
tremor. In an update to its October *World Economic
Outlook*, the International Monetary Fund draws special
attention to this failure to learn" (*Financial Times*, "The
Madness of Crowds," December 22, 1998).

In this editorial, the *Financial Times* uses the Dutch
tulipmania as the historical template for the global financial crisis of October 1998. How accurate is its interpretation of the tulipmania and of the statements of the
IMF's report? The Interim Report did discuss how risk
control works in the financial markets. Usually, when we
think of risk control, we do not think in terms of panic,

exuberance, or irrationality. We think of correct, prudent behavior on the part of financial institutions. Indeed, that was the gist of the Interim Report: standard risk control procedures require that when some disturbance hits, banks have to adjust their credit positions. It is exactly such prudent behavior that makes all the contagion of crises explainable. The thrust of the report was not that there was irrationality, panic, or mania. Rather, the report was a fundamental explanation of how the process worked, a documentation of the interconnections among financial markets. These risk control procedures are, in fact, *imposed* by industrial country regulators as a way of managing market and credit risk.

• "When the crowd tried to reverse direction after August 17, as Russia defaulted on its debt, many comforting systems for limiting risk broke down. This was because, like the seventeenth century tulip speculators, they relied on continuous orderly markets for closing unsuccessful positions. When everyone panicked the computerized strategies only exacerbated market turmoil" (*Financial Times*, "The Madness of Crowds," December 22, 1998).

I have spent a great deal of time studying the tulip speculation, and I have never seen any reference to tulip speculators' relying on continuously orderly markets. This is just something that the *Financial Times* editorial writer made up. There can be no more stark example of how the tulipmania episode is used: it is simply a rhetorical device to put across an argument. The story is now on such a mythological level that anyone feels the ability to embellish it, however falsely, to make a point.

For what reason is the tulipmania generally invoked? The argument is always that the existence of tulipmania proves that markets are crazy. A curious disturbance in a particular modern market can then be attributed to crazy behavior, so perhaps the market needs to be more severely regulated. Thus, these early episodes are the dream events for those who want to control the flow of capital.

The Famous Bubbles

History is a rhetorical weapon to be used in influencing modern policy outcomes. In particular, the invocation of bubbles is one such use of history. We now turn to the histories of the early bubbles to track down what they actually imply about the behavior of the private capital markets.

I aim here to supply market fundamental explanations for the three most famous bubbles: the Dutch tulipmania (1634–1637), the Mississippi Bubble (1719–1720), and the closely connected South Sea Bubble (1720). Though several authors have proposed market fundamental explanations for the well-documented Mississippi and South Sea Bubbles, these episodes are still treated in the modern view as spectacular outbursts of crowd irrationality. This interpretation is attributable to the influence of Charles Mackay's ([1841] 1852) famous descriptions of the frenzied speculative crowds that materialized in Paris and London in 1719 and 1720.

I concentrate most on the tulipmania because it is the event that most modern observers view as obviously crazy. I briefly discuss the historical background from which the tulipmania emerged, review the traditional version of the tulipmania, and trace the sources of the traditional version. To understand the nature of tulip markets, we must focus on how the reproductive cycle of the tulip itself determined behavior during the mania.

Data on seventeenth-century tulip prices and markets are too limited to construct "market fundamentals" on the supply and demand for tulip bulbs. I simply characterize the movement of prices for a variety of bulbs during and after the mania and compare the results to the pattern of price declines for initially rare eighteenth-century bulbs. This evidence can then be used to address the question of whether the seventeenth-century tulip speculation clearly exhibits the existence of a speculative mania.

I conclude that the most famous aspect of the mania, the extremely high prices reported for rare bulbs and their rapid decline, reflects normal pricing behavior in bulb markets and cannot be interpreted as evidence of market irrationality.

The Mississippi and South Sea Bubbles are the other two examples that appear on everyone's short list of spectacular financial collapses. They provide the most popular synonym for speculative mania. Based on the innovative economic theories of John Law, essentially what we now call Keynesian theories, both involved financial manipulations, monetary creation, and government connivance on a scale that was not matched again until this century, but which have now become commonplace. I will describe the nature of the asset markets and financial manipulations that occurred in these episodes and cast these also as market fundamentals.

II

The Tulipmania Legend

Gathered around the campfires early in their training, fledgling economists hear the legend of the Dutch tulip speculation from their elders, priming them with a skeptical attitude toward speculative markets. That prices of "intrinsically useless" bulbs could have risen so high and collapsed so rapidly seems to provide a decisive example of the instability and irrationality that may materialize in asset markets. The Dutch tulipmania of 1634–1637 always appears as a favorite case of speculative excess, even providing a synonym in our jargon for a speculative mania.

As a nonessential agricultural commodity, the tulip could have been reproduced rapidly and without limit, should its relative price have increased. Since market fundamental prices under any reasonable explanation should not have attained recorded levels, the tulipmania phenomenon has made it more likely that a sizable body of economists will occasionally embrace a rational or irrational "bubble hypothesis" in debates about whether bubbles have emerged in other episodes.

1   A Political and Economic Background

The introduction of the tulip market into the Netherlands and the tulipmania occurred in the midst of the Eighty Years' War of independence between the Dutch and the Spanish.[1] Spanish possession of the Low Countries had arisen through marriage; both the old Burgundian possessions in the Low Countries and Spain had been melded with Hapsburg territories in Central Europe in this manner. In trying to centralize and make organizational sense of this amalgamation of territories, the Hapsburgs attempted to impose administrative reforms that initiated the Dutch rebellion in 1567. This war was waged continuously, with Spain using the Spanish Netherlands (Belgium) as a base to attack the United Provinces until the Twelve Years' Truce was arranged in 1609. The Spanish were thwarted in their attempts to subjugate the Netherlands, which consolidated its territory and eventually seized control of most of international shipping. During this phase of the war, the English and Dutch formed an alliance, under which the English defeated of the Spanish Armada in 1588.

In 1618, the Thirty Years' War broke out in Europe, aligning the Hapsburgs and the Holy Roman Empire, including the Spanish, on the Catholic side against various Protestant powers in Central Europe. The Thirty Years' War was particularly destructive of the populations and economies of Central Europe, with many principalities in the Holy Roman Empire losing one-third of their populations. The map from Rich and Wilson (1975, 42) indicates the population declines to the east of the Netherlands in this period.

With the expiration of the Twelve Years' Truce in 1621, the Spanish-Dutch Eighty Years' War revived as a continuing parallel of the Thirty Years' War and did not end until just before the general peace of 1648. In every year of the war, the Dutch fielded armies as large as 100,000 men during campaigning seasons and supported large fleets, though the population of the Netherlands was no more than 1.5 million. The Dutch provided much of the strategic planning and finance for the Protestant effort, with France negotiating and financing the successive interventions of Denmark and Sweden on the Protestant side in the 1620s and 1630s.

From 1620 to 1645, the Dutch established near monopolies on trade with the East Indies and Japan, conquered most of Brazil, took possession of the Dutch Caribbean islands, and founded New York. In 1628, the Dutch West India Company captured in a Caribbean naval action the

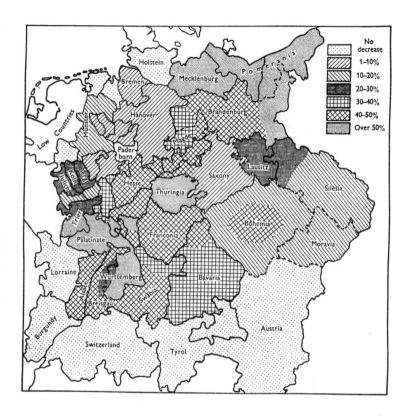

entire year's output of silver and gold from Spain's
American possessions, amounting to between 11.5 and 14
million guilders, or about $90 million in today's gold
prices.[2] In 1635, the Dutch formed a military alliance with
Richelieu's France, which eventually placed the Spanish
Netherlands in a precarious position. In 1639, the Dutch
completely destroyed a second Spanish Armada of a size
comparable to that of 1588. As an outcome of the war,

Spain ceased to be the dominating power in Europe, and the Netherlands, though small in population and resources, became a major power center because of its complete control over international trade and international finance. The Dutch were to seventeenth-century trade and finance as the British were to nineteenth-century trade and finance.

Of course, this period was not one of uninterrupted triumph. Notably, in the years 1634–1637, the Dutch suffered several setbacks. From 1635 to 1637, the bubonic plague ravaged the Netherlands. In July 1634, the Empire completely defeated Swedish forces in the Battle of Nordlingen, forcing a treaty on the German Protestant principalities in the May 1635 Peace of Prague and releasing Spanish resources for the war against the Dutch. Along with the growing war weariness in the Netherlands, these events forced France to enter the Thirty Years' War militarily with the Dutch alliance in 1635. Initially unprepared, the French suffered major setbacks, culminating in an Imperial invasion of northern France in August 1636. The war did not again turn in favor of the Dutch until the capture of the important Spanish fortress of Breda in October 1637.

The expansion of Dutch political power depended on the rapid development of the Dutch economy. The Netherlands was a largely urbanized society engaged in manufacture, trade, and finance; the rest of Europe consisted of peasant societies. The major Dutch industries were shipbuilding, fisheries, transport, textiles, and finance. During the seventeenth century, most ships in European merchant fleets were built by the Dutch; and the Dutch merchant fleet outnumbered the fleets of all the other maritime nations of Europe combined. The Dutch dominated transport in grains, precious and common metals, and salt and other bulk goods; as an entrepôt, the Netherlands provided a natural location for European markets in all major commodities.

Sophisticated finance mechanisms evolved with the establishment of the commodity markets. Amsterdam became the dominant market for short- and long-term credit; and markets in stocks, commodity futures, and options materialized early in the seventeenth century.[3] Trading of national loans of many countries centered in Amsterdam, as did a market in the shares of joint stock companies. The East India Company, founded in 1602, gradually gained control over East Asian trade and consistently paid out large dividends. The West India Company, founded in 1622, was given the right to undertake ventures in the Western Hemisphere, including the incipient takeover of the Atlantic slave trade.

At the time of the tulip speculation, the Netherlands was a highly commercialized country with well-developed and innovative financial markets and a large population of sophisticated traders. Its participation in innumerable risky ventures had proven so successful that the era is considered the golden age of the Netherlands.

2

The Traditional Image of Tulipmania

Descriptions of the tulip speculation always are framed in a context of doubt about how the Dutch, usually so astute in their speculations, could have been caught in such an obvious blunder. Modern references to the episode depend on the brief description in Mackay ([1841] 1852). The tulip originated in Turkey but diffused into Western Europe only in the middle of the sixteenth century, carried first to Austria by a fancier of the flower. The tulip was immediately accepted by the wealthy as a beautiful and rare flower, appropriate for the most stylish gardens. The market was for durable bulbs, not flowers. As in so many other markets, the Dutch dominated that for tulips, initiating the development of methods to create new flower varieties. The bulbs that commanded high prices produced unique, beautifully patterned flowers; common tulips were sold at much lower prices.

Beginning in 1634, nonprofessionals entered the tulip trade in large numbers. According to Mackay, individual bulb prices reached enormous levels. For example, a single Semper Augustus bulb was sold at the height of the speculation for 5500 guilders, a weight of gold equal to $33,000 evaluated at $300/oz. Mackay provided neither the sources of these bulb prices nor the dates on which they were observed, however.

Mackay emphasized the lunacy of the event through a pair of anecdotes about a sailor who mistakenly ate valuable bulbs and an unsuspecting English traveler who experimented with them by peeling off their layers. The implausibility of a Dutch businessman leaving a highly valuable bulb lying about for a loutish sailor to eat for lunch or for a presumptuous English experimenter to dissect escaped him. He also described some barter transactions for acquiring rare bulbs so that the monetary expenditure could be translated into units of goods more meaningful to the modern (1841) reader.

Mackay then shifted to the final speculative frenzy, stating that large amounts of foreign funds entered the country to add to the speculation, and people from all classes hurriedly liquidated other assets to participate in the tulip market. However, he presented no evidence of the sources and quantity of these foreign funds.

Finally and inexplicably, the frenzy terminated; and, overnight, even rare bulbs could find no buyers at 10 percent of their previous prices, creating a long-term economic distress, according to Mackay. No evidence of immediate post-collapse transaction prices of the rare bulbs was produced by Mackay, however. Rather, Mackay cited prices from bulb sales from 60 years, 130 years, or 200 years later as indicators of the magnitude of the collapse and of the obvious misalignment of prices at the peak of the speculation. Moreover, Mackay provided no evidence of the general economic context from which the speculation emerged.

Where Does the Tulipmania Legend Come From?

Given its strategic position in current views of tulipmania, it is vital to investigate from which sources Mackay constructed his version of the speculation. While at one point Mackay includes a minor citation to Johann Beckmann, he plagiarized most of his description from Beckmann with a little literary embellishment.[4]

Beckmann, the original source of the sailor and dissector anecdotes referred to in the previous chapter, cites Blainville (1743) as his source for the story about the Englishman. A careful reading of Blainville, however, turns up only a one-sentence report that a tulip speculation occurred from 1634–1637 in what is otherwise a baroque travel log of Haarlem. Indeed, Blainville's description of his travels through Holland was a diary of a tour made in 1705, seventy years after the speculation. For the sailor story, Beckmann mentions that the incident occurred while John Balthasar Schuppe (1610–1661) was in Holland, without other reference. However, the context of the paragraph in which the story appears seems to indicate that it happened after the tulip speculation. Mackay, who greatly dramatizes both stories, cites Blainville as the source for both, obviously without having researched beyond Beckmann's accounts.

Beckmann carefully reported his sources of information about the functioning of the markets and bulb sales prices, using notably the dialogues between two fictional characters Gaergoedt and Waermondt ("Samenspraeck Tusschen Waermondt ende Gaergoedt: Flora," 1637), hereafter denoted G&W, and Munting's (1672, 1696) discussions of this episode. G&W is a series of three pamphlets in dialogue form that provides details about the markets and numerous prices of various bulbs, taken mostly from the final day of the speculation. These pamphlets were motivated by a moralistic attack against speculation by the authorities, as were all of the numerous pamphlets that appeared immediately after the end of the episode.[5]

Munting was a botanist who wrote a 1000-folio volume on numerous flowers. Though Mackay claims that the entire volume was devoted to the tulipmania, only the six pages allocated to tulips discuss the episode. Mackay must have recorded Beckmann's reference to Munting without examining the Munting text at all. All the price data described in Munting can be found in the G&W dialogues, so we must conclude that this also is Munting's primary source.

The popular version of the tulipmania, to the extent that it is based on scholarly work, follows a lattice of hearsay fanning out from the G&W dialogues.

A more careful line of research has had little impact on our current interpretation of the tulip speculation. Solms-Laubach's (1899) history of tulips in Europe provides an extensive description of the available literature on tulips, including the G&W dialogues. Most of his price data originates in G&W, but he also explores records left by notaries of tulip contracts written during the mania.

Van Damme documented the tulipmania in a series of short articles written from 1899 to 1903.[6] This series consists of reprints of G&W, reproductions of some pre-collapse pricing contracts, and details of bulb auctions from just before the collapse and from six years after the end of the speculation. Since many of the prices in G&W are also on the earlier auction list, it provides a key confirmation of the validity of the prices in the G&W dialogues.

Posthumus (1927, 1929, 1934), the only economist in this literature, extended the available data by compiling and reproducing more of the notaries' contracts. Most of his discussion, however, again depends on price information in the G&W dialogues and on information compiled by Van Damme.

Finally, Krelage (1942, 1946) extensively describes the markets, though the prices that he reports for the speculation period also seem to come from G&W. Krelage (1946) does provide tulip price lists from sales in 1708 and 1709 and a 1739 bulb catalogue. In addition, he compiles a time series of prices for a large variety of hyacinth bulbs during the eighteenth and nineteenth centuries.

Even this line of research accomplishes little more than gathering additional price data, and those data that we have are not organized in a systematic time series. Posthumus attempts to analyze the functioning of the futures markets that materialized at the end of the speculation. But in spite of his efforts, we have inherited the concept of the tulipmania as the most famous of bubbles, accompanied by no serious effort to describe what might constitute the market fundamentals of the bulb market.

4

Establishment Attitudes toward Futures Markets and Short Selling: The Source of the Pamphlets

In his history of the Dutch Golden Age, Schama (1987) discusses the forces that led to the successful development of the Dutch economy in the seventeenth century.[7] He structures his description around a perceived tension in the ruling oligarchy between "speculation" and safe "investment." The oligarchy and its magistrates sought a balance between "safe" and "unsafe" areas of economic activity, knowing that sustained economic well-being depended on secure enterprises while growth depended on a willingness to undertake risky new ventures.

Safe areas of economic and financial activity were those regulated by public authorities such as the City Chamber of Marine Insurance, the Wisselbank, and the trade in commodities through the Baltic Sea, which the Dutch effectively monopolized. Riskier though still vital areas of economic activity were the more distant trades in the hands of the Dutch East India Company and the Dutch West India Company. The East India Company was enormously successful, earning large profits for its shareholders. The West India Company, more an instrument in the military contest with Spain and Portugal, performed poorly.

Trading activity in company shares on the bourse was yet a riskier financial activity. Such trades involved spot transactions, stock options, and futures trades. Soon after active trading in East India Company shares was initiated in 1606, organized bear raids were conducted on share prices under the direction of the noted speculator Isaac Le Maire. These involved short sales of stock and the spreading of negative rumors about the affairs of the company, a tactic employed to this day.

Reaction to these practices led to an edict in 1610 that prohibited such manipulative activities. Most notably for our purposes, the edict banned "windhandel" or "trading in the wind," trading in shares not currently possessed by the seller. Sales for future delivery were permitted to people who actually owned shares. Future sales that were not obviously for such hedging purposes were prohibited. The authorities continually regarded futures trading as immoral gambling, and the edict was reiterated and extended with the renewal of war with Spain in 1621, again in 1630, and most notably in the midst of the tulipmania in 1636.

The authorities did not prosecute people for participating in proscribed futures contracts. They simply refused legal enforcement of such contracts. In a process known as "an appeal to Frederick" (the Stadholder or

Prince), a buyer of a prohibited futures contract could repudiate it with the backing of the courts. Thus, the futures trades and short sales frowned upon by the authorities could continue as long as contracts could be privately enforced. A repudiation might lead to the exclusion of an established trader from the bourse and a consequent loss of trading profits in the future, so a buyer would not likely repudiate a moderate loss on a futures contract. If the loss were sufficient to bankrupt and impoverish a trader, he would be likely to repudiate however.

To the authorities, the tulip speculation represented an obviously unsafe financial speculation in which a legitimate business had suddenly degenerated into a bizarre form of gambling. The futures trading, which was the center of the activity, was clearly banned by the edicts; and in the end, the courts did not enforce deals made in the taverns where such trading occurred, all of which were repudiated. It is incomprehensible that anyone involved in the fluctuating associations of the taverns would have entered such unenforceable agreements in the first place unless they were merely part of a game.

According to Schama, the speculation frightened the Dutch elite with a demonstration of how quickly a seemingly safe activity could convert itself into undisciplined gambling: "It was, in their view, money run amok—a kind of anarchy in which all the conventions and rules for virtuous and sober commercial conduct had been thrown to the wind" (p. 359).

The ruling elite implemented a propaganda drive against such behavior, described by Shama as follows:

The magistrates of the Dutch towns saw niceties of equity as less pressing than the need to de-intoxicate the tulip craze. . . . But they still felt impelled to launch a didactic campaign in tracts, sermons, and prints against the folly, since its special wickedness had been leading the common people astray. To the humanist oligarchs, the tulip mania had violated all their most sacred tenets: moderation, prudence, discretion, right reason and reciprocity between effort and reward. (Pp. 361–362)

The objectives of this campaign were to channel speculative proclivities into the safe areas of economic activity. Not surprisingly, the safe areas coincided with those controlled by the ruling elite. Among the numerous antispeculative pamphlets launched during this reaction were the G&W dialogues.

5

The Bubonic Plague

External to the bulb market, one extraordinary event in the period 1634–1637 may have driven the speculation. From 1635 to 1637, the bubonic plague ravaged the Netherlands, killing 17,193 people in Amsterdam alone in 1636 (one-seventh of the population). It also caused 14,502 deaths in Leiden in 1635 (33 percent of the 1622 population); and it killed 14 percent of the population of Haarlem, the center of the tulip speculation, from August to November 1636, the moment when the trading in common and cheap varieties took off.

The plague had marched westward with the dynamics of the armies in Germany starting in 1630.[8] Plague also broke out from 1623 to 1625, from 1654 to 1655, and from 1663 to 1664, killing in Amsterdam one-ninth, one-eighth, and one-sixth of the population, respectively.

Van Damme (1976) quotes C. de Koning, who states that the plague began in 1635 and forced the city authorities to take drastic health measures:

These and other precautions could not prevent the progress of the outbreak that caused 5723 to die during August, September, October and November, 1636, so many that the number of graveyards was too small. So great was the misery and sorrow of citizens and inhabitants that the best description would only be a weak image of the great misery of those unhappy days, which is why we will end the story by thanking the almighty God for saving us from this great terror from which our forefathers suffered so much. In the midst of all this misery that made our city suffer, people were caught by a special fever, by a particular anxiety to get rich in a very short period of time. The means to this were thought to be found in the tulip trade. This trade, so well known in the history of our country, and so well developed in our city should be taught to our fellow citizens as a proof of forefatherly folly. (Pp. 129–130)

Of the plague in Haarlem, Van Damme notes that "one can presume that the tulip futures speculation reached its peak when the plague was worst." De Vries (1976) claims that the plague outbreak of 1635–1636 "perhaps by spreading a certain fatalism among the population kicked off the most frenzied episode of the mania" (226).

The population of the Netherlands faced an increased probability of imminent death, either from plague or Spanish invasion, from 1635 to 1637, coincident with the tulip speculation, and a decline in the probability afterward. Although the plague outbreak may be a false clue, it is conceivable that a gambling binge tied, as we will see, to a drinking game emerged as a response to the death threat.

6   The Broken Tulip

An understanding of the tulip markets requires some information about the nature of the tulip. A bulb flower, the tulip can propagate either through seeds or through buds that form on the mother bulb. Properly cultivated, the buds can directly reproduce another bulb. Each bulb, after planting, eventually disappears during the growing season. By the end of the season, the original bulb is replaced by a clone, the primary bud, which is now a functioning bulb, and by a few secondary buds. Asexual reproduction through buds, the principal propagation method, produces an increase in bulbs at a maximum annual rate of from 100 to 150 percent in normal bulbs.[9]

A bulb produced directly from seed requires seven to twelve years before it flowers. The flowers appear in April or May and last for about a week. The amount of time required before the secondary buds flower depends on the size of the bulb produced from the bud. Hartman and Kester (1983) state that the time before flowering of a bulb less than 5 cm. in diameter is three years, of a bulb from 5 to 7 cm. is two years, and of a bulb greater than 8 cm. is one year.

In June, bulbs can be removed from their beds but must be replanted by September. To verify the delivery of a specific variety, spot trading in bulbs had to occur immediately after the flowering period, usually in June.

Tulips are subject to invasion by a mosaic virus whose important effect, called "breaking," is to produce remarkable patterns on the flower, some of which are considered beautiful. The pattern imposed on a particular flower cannot be reproduced through seed propagation; seeds will produce bulbs that yield a common flower, since they are unaffected by the virus. These bulbs may themselves eventually "break" at some unknown date but into a pattern that may not be remarkable. A specific pattern can be reproduced by cultivating the buds into new bulbs.

As another effect, the mosaic virus makes the bulb sickly and reduces its rate of reproduction. Although seventeenth-century florists thought that breaking was a normal stage in the maturing process of breeder bulbs (the stock of bulbs vulnerable to attack by the virus), theories arose that broken tulips were diseased. For example, La Chesnee Monstereul (1654), contrasting the theory of breaking as "self perfection" with a disease theory, noted that broken bulbs had smaller bulb and stem sizes and that they never produced more than three buds.

Smith (1937, 413) states that broken bulbs do not "proliferate as freely" as undiseased plants but that this weakening need not cause broken bulbs to succumb, giving as an example the broken Zomerschoon, which has been actively cultivated since 1620. Van Slogteren (1960) claims that the mosaic virus may cause total loss of a plant or a 10–20 percent reduction in propagation rates.

Almost all bulbs traded in the tulipmania have by now completely disappeared. For example, the Royal General Bulbgrowers Society's (1969) classification of thousands of actively grown tulips mentions such important bulbs of the tulip speculation as Admirael Liefkens, Admirael van der Eyck, Paragon Liefkens, Semper Augustus, and Viceroy only as historically important names. The only bulbs still grown were the Gheele Croonen and Lack van Rijn, despised in the 1630s as common flowers except at the height of the speculation. Currently, even these bulbs are grown only by collectors.

The high market prices for tulips, to which the current version of the tulipmania refers, were for particularly beautiful broken bulbs. Single-colored breeder bulbs, except to the extent that they could potentially break, were not valued; and all important tulip varieties in the first two centuries of European cultivation were diseased. Broken bulbs fell from fashion only in the nineteenth century.[10] Indeed, since breaking was unpredictable, some have characterized tulipmania among growers as a gamble, with growers "vying to produce better and more bizarre variegations and feathering."[11]

Though it is now known that the mosaic virus is spread by aphids, methods of encouraging breaking were not well understood in the seventeenth century. G&W

suggested grafting half a bulb of a broken tulip to half a bulb of an unbroken tulip to cause breaking (van Slogteren 1960, 27). La Chesnee Monstereul (1654, 163) states that the art of "speeding transformation" was controversial among florists. D'Ardene (1760, 198–217) devotes a chapter to breaking in tulips, shedding little light on methods to encourage breaking.

7 The Bulb Market, 1634–1637

The market for bulbs was limited to professional growers until 1634, but participation encompassed a more general class of speculators by the end of 1634. A rising demand for bulbs in France apparently drove the speculation.

In France, it became fashionable for women to array quantities of fresh tulips at the tops of their gowns. Wealthy men competed to present the most exotic flowers to eligible women, thereby driving up the demand for rare flowers. Munting (1696, 911) claims that at the time of the speculation, a single *flower* of a particular broken tulip was sold for 1000 guilders in Paris. This was a final demand price for a consumption good and not the asset price of the bulb.

Market participants could make many types of deals. The rare flowers were called "piece" goods, and particular bulbs were sold by their weight. The heavier bulbs had more outgrowths and therefore represented a collection of future bulbs. The weight standard was the "aas," about one-twentieth of a gram. For example, if a Gouda of 57 azen (plural of aas) were sold for a given price, the sale contract would refer to a particular bulb planted at a given location. Once markets developed in common bulbs, they were sold in standardized units of 1000 azen or 1 pound (9728 azen in Haarlem, 10,240 azen in Amsterdam). Purchase contracts for "pound" goods would not refer to particular bulbs.

A purchase between September and June was necessarily a contract for future delivery. Also, markets materialized for the outgrowths of the rarer bulbs. The outgrowths could not be delivered immediately, as they had to attain some minimum size before they could be separated from the parent bulb to assure the viability of the new bulb. Hence, the contracts for outgrowths were also for future delivery.

Formal futures markets developed in 1636 and were the primary focus of trading before the collapse in February 1637. Earlier deals had employed written contracts entered into before a notary. Trading became extensive enough in the summer of 1636—the peak of the plague— that traders began meeting in numerous taverns in groups called "colleges" where trades were regulated by a few rules governing the method of bidding and fees. Buyers were required to pay one-half stuiver (1 stuiver = 1/20 guilder) out of each contracted guilder to sellers up to a maximum of 3 guilders for each deal for "wine money." To the extent that a trader ran a balanced book over any length of time, these payments would cancel out. No margin was required from either party, so bankruptcy constraints did not restrict the magnitude of an individual's position.

Typically, the buyer did not currently possess the cash to be delivered on the settlement date, and the seller did not currently possess the bulb. Neither party intended a delivery on the settlement date; only a payment of the difference between the contract and settlement price was expected. So, as a bet on the price of the bulbs on the settlement date, this market was not different in function from currently operating futures markets. The operational differences were that the contracts were not continuously marked to market—that is, repriced according to daily price fluctuations, required no margin deposits to guarantee compliance, and consisted of commitments of individuals rather than of an exchange. A collapse would require the untangling of gross, rather than net, positions.

All discussions of the tulipmania openly criticize the activity of buying or selling for future delivery without current possession of the commodity sold or an intention to effect delivery. They attack futures markets as a means of creating artificial risk and do not consider their role in marketing existing risks.

It is unclear which date was designated as the settlement date in the "college" contracts. No bulbs were delivered under the deals struck in the new futures markets in 1636–1637 prior to the collapse because of the necessity of waiting until June to exhume the bulbs. It is also unclear how the settlement price was determined.

Beckmann (1846, 29) states that the settlement price was "determined by that at which most bargains were made," presumably at the time of expiration of a given contract. Again, this is the standard practice in current futures markets.

Serious and wealthy tulip fanciers who traded regularly in rare varieties did not participate in the new speculative markets. Even after the collapse of the speculation, they continued to trade rare bulbs for "large amounts."[12] To the extent that rare bulbs also traded on the futures markets, this implies that no one arbitraged the spot and futures markets. Taking a long position in spot bulbs required substantial capital resources or access to the financial credit markets. To hedge this position with a short sale in the futures market would have required the future purchaser to have substantial capital or access to sound credit; substantial risk of noncompliance with the deal in the futures market would have undermined the hedge. Since participants in the futures markets faced no capital requirements, there was no basis for an arbitrage.

During most of the period of the tulip speculation, high prices and recorded trading occurred only for the rare bulbs. Common bulbs did not figure in the speculation until November 1636.

Posthumus (1929, 444) hypothesizes the following timing of events:

I think the sequence of events may be seen as follows. At the end of 1634, the new nonprofessional buyers came into action.

Towards the middle of 1635 prices rose rapidly, while people could buy on credit, generally delivering at once some article of value; at the same time the sale per aas was introduced. About the middle of 1636 the colleges appeared; and soon thereafter the trade in non-available bulbs was started, while in November of the same year the trade was extended to the common varieties, and bulbs were sold by the thousand azen and per pound.

8

Some Characterization of the Data

To a great extent, the available price data are a blend of apples and oranges. I cannot separate the prices determined in the colleges, in which bankruptcy constraints seem not to have been imposed, from those that may have been more seriously binding on the transactors. Moreover, I cannot separate the spot from the futures deals, although all transactions after September 1636 must have been for future delivery. One natural way to separate these categories is to split the sample between "piece" goods and "pound" goods. Posthumus claims that there was a class difference between those trading in piece goods and those trading in pound goods, even in the colleges. Members of the middle classes and capitalized workers such as the weavers disdained the pound goods and traded only in the rarer bulbs.

In charts 1 through 16, I depict the "time series" in guilders/aas or guilders/bulb that I have been able to reconstruct for various bulbs. These charts consist of data gathered from auctions, contracts recorded with notaries,

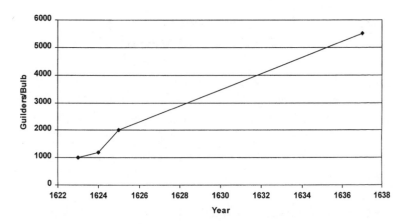

Chart 1
Semper Augustus

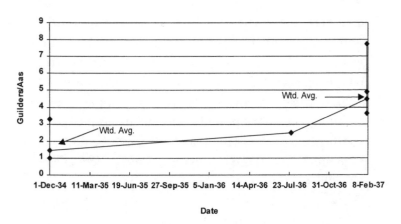

Chart 2
Admirael van der Eyck

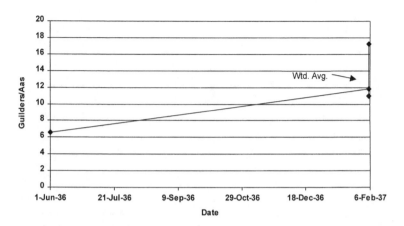

Chart 3
Admirael Liefkens

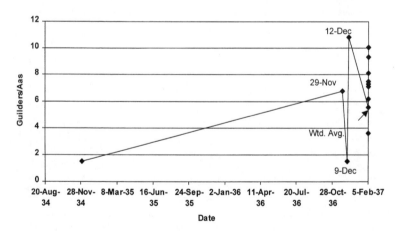

Chart 4
Gouda mature bulbs

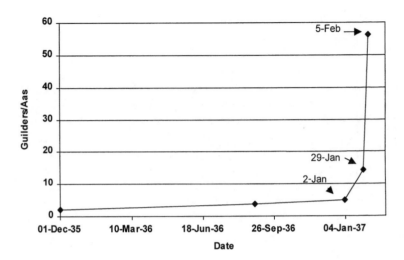

Chart 5
Gouda buds

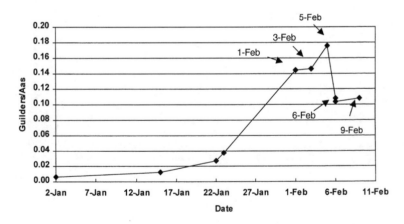

Chart 6
Switsers

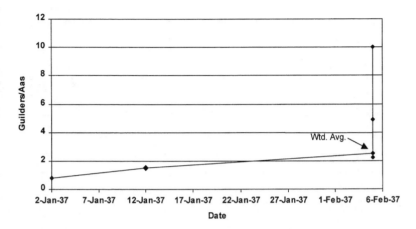

Chart 7
Scipio

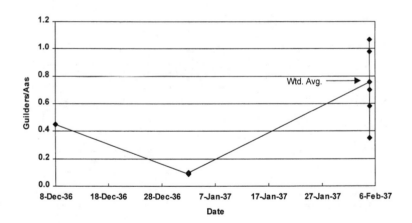

Chart 8
Gheele ende Roote van Leyden

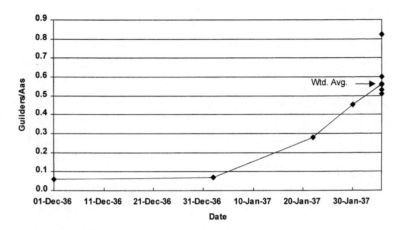

Chart 9
Oudenaerden

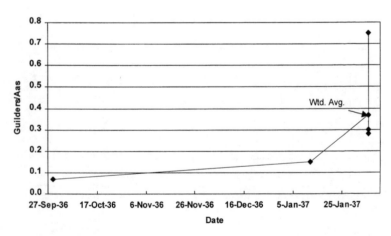

Chart 10
Groote Geplumiceerde

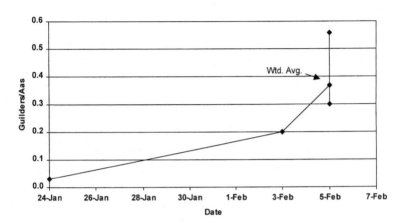

Chart 11
Macx

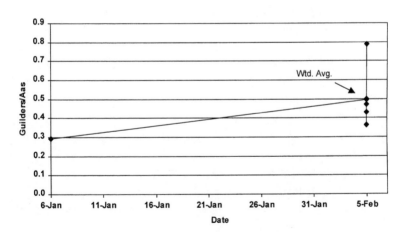

Chart 12
Nieuwberger

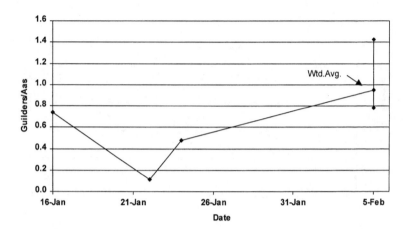

Chart 13
Le Grand

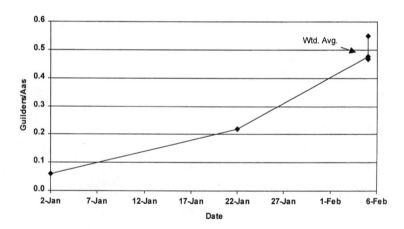

Chart 14
Coorenaerts

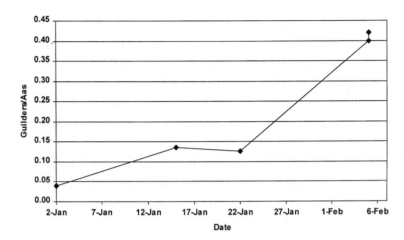

Chart 15
Centen

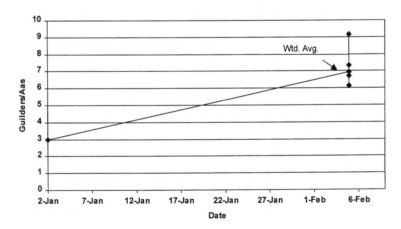

Chart 16
Viceroy

and the G&W dialogues. Data for Oudenaerden, Scipio, Nieuwberger, Macx, Groote Geplumiceerde, Coorenaerts, Centen, Witte Croonen, Gheele ende Roote van Leyden, and Switsers are in terms of guilders/aas for standardized weights of pound goods. Data for Semper Augustus, Admirael van der Eyck, Admirael Liefkens, Viceroy, and Gouda, are for individual bulbs that vary in weight from one to many hundred azen. Chart 4 indicates prices for mature Gouda bulbs; chart 5 is for Gouda of very low weights, ranging from 1 to 7 aas, which I have interpreted as bud prices.

The last observations for each series, except for the Switsers, were recorded on February 5, 1637, apparently the peak of the mania. For that date, there are usually several price observations for each flower, but their order of appearance in the charts has no meaning. Specifically, the charts do not indicate a price explosion at an infinite rate on February 5. I have connected the price lines to the weighted average of prices for February 5.

The bulbs that can be included among "piece" goods are Admirael Liefkens, Admirael van der Eyck, Gouda, Semper Augustus, and Viceroy. Among these, the Gouda can be considered a standard, since we have the longest price series for this bulb, starting at the beginning of the speculation. The bulbs that can be included among the "pound" goods, that is, bulbs trading in 1000 aasen or pound lots are Centen, Coorenaerts, Gheele ende Roote van Leyden, Groote Geplumiceerde, Le Grand, Macx, Nieuwburger, Oudenaerden, Switsers, and Witte

Croonen.[13] Other bulbs are more difficult to classify, encompassing different deals in which either odd weights or standard weights appear.

Generally, the pound goods sold at much lower prices per aas than the piece goods. However, in the last few months of the speculation—at the time of the outbreak of plague in Haarlem—their prices increased much more rapidly than did those of the piece goods. Prices of Coorenaerts, Gheele ende Roote van Leyden, Le Grand, Macx, Oudenaerden, Switsers, and Witte Croonen rose up to twentyfold within one month. Over a much longer period, the prices of the piece goods doubled or perhaps tripled.

The exception to the relatively slow price movement for rarer bulbs is for the prices of Gouda buds shown in chart 5. Apparently, buds attracted speculation of the same sort as the common varieties. However, the very sharp rise comes from a single observation of 56 guilders per aas for a 4 aas bulb on the last day of the speculation, February 5. Through January 29, the price data for Gouda buds were about the same as for mature bulbs—14 guilders per aas on January 29 and 5 guilders per aas on January 2 for buds compared to mature bulb prices of 10.8 guilders per aas on December 12 and a range between 3.6 and 10 guilders per aas on February 5. This fourfold increase in Gouda bud price is of the same order of magnitude as the price jumps for several of the common bulbs in the last week or two of the speculation—for example, Switser, Centen, and Macx.

9   Post-Collapse Tulip Prices

The tulip speculation collapsed after the first week of February 1637, but there is no explanation for this timing. A general suspension of settlement occurred on contracts coming due—that is, contracts were not rolled over.

On February 24, 1637, delegates of florists meeting in Amsterdam proposed that sales of tulips contracted on or before November 30, 1636 should be executed. For later contracts, the buyer would be given the right to reject the deal *on payment of 10 percent of the sale price* to the seller. This may be the source of the claims in Mackay that bulbs could not sell at 10 percent of their peak prices. The authorities did not adopt this suggestion.

On April 27, 1637, the States of Holland decided to suspend all contracts, giving the seller of existing bulbs the right to sell contracted bulbs at market prices during the suspension. The buyer in the contract would be responsible for the difference between this market price and whatever price the authorities eventually deter-mined for contract settlement. This decision released the growers to market the bulbs that would emerge in June.

The disposition of further settlement then becomes murky. Posthumus (1929, 446–447) states that many cities followed the example of Haarlem where in May 1638, the city council passed a regulation permitting buyers to terminate a contract on payment of 3.5 percent of the contract price.

Even the pre-collapse legal status of the futures contracts was unclear. Early price manipulation and bear raids in East India Company shares led to legal bans on short sales on the Amsterdam exchange in 1610. Whether the ban applied to traders on the new tulip futures market is unclear. Ultimately, the courts did not uphold any contracts for tulips, but local attempts at settlement were made.

With the end of large-scale bulb trading after February 1637, records of transaction prices virtually disappeared. Prices no longer were publicly recorded, and only an occasional estate auction of an important florist would reveal the magnitude of prices. Prior to 1634, only a handful of prices are available from recorded sales contracts: a pair of bulbs from 1612 reported by Posthumus (1929) in his contract numbers 3 and 4; a 1625 sale of three bulbs; and a 1633 sale of a pair of bulbs, both reported in Posthumus (1934). Even the series in chart 1 for the Semper Augustus is based on undocumented stories emanating from the historical authority Wassenaer in the 1620s, as reported by Solms-Laubach (1899, 77), among others.

Fortunately, van Damme (1976, 109–113) reports prices from a post-collapse estate auction in 1643. In the estate auction of the bulb dealer J. van Damme (no relation), fl. 42,013 were raised through the sale of bulbs. This amount reflects a bulb value comparable to the fl. 68,553 derived from the February 1637 estate auction from which we have received most of the tulipmania peak price data.

This total was not broken down into individual bulb prices. For those few bulbs sold in which the estate held a fractional interest, however, the sales prices were reported (van Damme 1976, 111). The prices were as follows:

1 Tulpa Meerman	fl. 430
1 Vrouge Brantson	fl. 25
1 General Rotgans	fl. 138
1 Verspreijt	fl. 582
1 Vroege Brantson	
$\frac{1}{4}$ of 1 English Admiral	

In addition, the records detailing the settling of the estate's accounts contains a list of 1643 cash expenditures for bulbs purchased in 1642. These prices were as follows:

$\frac{1}{2}$ pound Witte Croonen	fl. 37 st. 10
1 Admirael van der Eyck	fl. 225
1 English Admiral outgrowth	
1 English Admiral	fl. 210

Table 9.1
Post-Collapse Bulb Prices in Guilders

Bulb	Jan. 1637	Feb. 5, 1637	1642 or 1643	Annual % Depreciation[1]
1. Witte Croonen (one-half pound)	64.	1668. (avg.)	37.5	76
2. English Admiral (bulb)		700. (25 aas bulb)	210.	24
3. Admirael van der Eyck (bulb)		1345. (wtd. avg.)	220.*	36
4. General Rotgans (Rotgansen)		805. (1000 azen)	138.	35

*Adjusted downward fl. 5 to account for the English Admiral outgrowth.
[1] From February 1637 peak.

Individual bulbs then could still command high prices six years after the collapse. Four bulbs whose prices were listed individually also appear among the bulbs traded in 1636–1637: Witte Croonen, English Admiral, Admirael van der Eyck, and General Rotgans (Rotgansen). Witte Croonen were pound goods, and the others were piece goods. Table 9.1 presents a comparison of 1636, 1637, and 1642 or 1643 prices.

Even from the peaks of February 1637, the price declines of the rarer bulbs, English Admiral, Admiral van der Eyck, and General Rotgans, over the course of six years was not unusually rapid. We shall see below that they fit the pattern of decline typical of a prized variety.

10

Bulb Prices in Later Centuries

Eighteenth-Century Tulip Prices

Though a few prices are available from the years immediately after the collapse, a gap of about seventy years
arises in detailed tulip price data. While price data disappeared, at least the names of the important tulips
from the speculation remained current thirty-two years
after the collapse. Van der Groen (1669) mentions the
important tulips that a fashionable garden might hold.
Among them were Vroege Bleyenberger, Parragon
Grebber, Gheel and Roote van Leyden, Admirael van
Enchuysen, Brabanson, Senecours, Admirael de Man,
Coorenaerts, Jan Gerritz, Gouda, Saeyblom, Switsers,
Parragon Liefkens, and Semper Augustus.

High tulip prices are available only for much later
periods, and these are an order of magnitude lower
than those quoted during the speculation. Van Damme
(1976) reproduces numerous announcements of bulb
sales and auctions printed in such periodicals as the

Table 10.1
Guilder Prices of Tulip Bulbs Common to 1637, 1722, and 1739 Price
Lists

Bulb	Jan. 2, 1637	Feb. 5, 1637	1722	1739
1. Admirael de Man	18.	209.		0.1
2. Gheele Croonen	0.41	20.5		0.025*
3. Witte Croonen	2.2	57.		0.02*
4. Gheele ende Roote van Leyden	17.5	136.5	0.1	0.2
5. Switsers	1.	30.	0.05	
6. Semper Augustus	2000. (7/1/25)	6290.		0.1
7. Zomerschoon		480.	0.15	0.15
8. Admirael van Enchuysen		4900.	0.2	
9. Fama		776.	0.03*	
10. Admirael van Hoorn		65.5	0.1	
11. Admirael Liefkens		2968.	0.2	

Note: To construct this table, I have assumed a standard bulb size of
175 azen. All sales by the bulb are assumed to be in the standard
weight, and prices are adjusted proportionally from reported prices.
When more than one bulb price is available on a given day, I report
the average of adjusted prices.
*Sold in lots of 100 bulbs.

Haarlemscher Courant in the latter half of the seventeenth
century, but there is no record of prices generated in the
auctions.

Table 10.1 reports prices for bulbs from January 2, 1637;
February 5, 1637; 1722; and 1739. These prices come from
several sources. Krelage (1946) reproduces tulip lists from

auctions on May 17, 1707, in the Hague (542) and on May 16, 1708, in Rotterdam (541), on which a participant fortuitously annotated the final sales prices. While the 1707 auction list contains eighty-four different bulb names and that of 1708 contains twelve, no bulb name of the hundreds commonly traded in 1637 appears in the lists. Krelage reproduces only the first page of the 1708 price list. The entire list was sold to British buyers with the breakup of Krelage's library, and I have been unable to examine it.

Bradley (1728) reproduces the 1722 bulb catalogue of a Haarlem florist. The majority of the hundreds of bulbs in this catalogue were offered at prices less than one guilder, and only one, Superintendent Roman, sold for 100 guilders. The list, however, does contain prices for twenty-five bulbs that appeared in the 1637 tulip speculation.

Krelage (1946) also reproduces a 1739 Haarlem price catalogue of hyacinth and tulip bulbs. Of its several hundred different bulbs, only six names match those of bulbs traded in 1637. Interestingly, it offers Semper Augustus bulbs for 0.1 guilders.

Even starting in January 1637, before the peak of the speculation, the price decline is remarkable. Prices fall to levels of 1 percent, 0.5 percent, 0.1 percent, or 0.005 percent of the January 1637 values over a century. Also noteworthy is the convergence of prices of all individually sold bulbs to a common value, regardless of the initial bulb values.

Table 10.2 contains prices of bulbs common to the 1707 auction and either the 1722 or the 1739 price lists. While this was not a period known for a tulip speculation or crash, prices display the same pattern of decline. Bulbs appearing on an auction list were for recently developed rare varieties that commanded relatively high prices. None of the bulbs on the 1739 list carried a price greater than eight guilders, while most prices were much lower. Rare and valuable bulbs would not have appeared on a standard dealer's list. Conversely, auctions would not have bothered with common, inexpensive bulbs. Because the 1637 rare bulbs had become common by 1707, it is not surprising that their names had disappeared from auction lists.

By the time they appeared in a general catalogue, they had diffused sufficiently to become relatively common. Again, in thirty-two years, prices declined to 3 percent, 0.25 percent, 0.35 percent, or 0.04 percent of their original values, repeating the pattern of decline of the bulbs from the tulipmania. Indeed, the valuable bulbs of 1707 even converged approximately to the same prices as the valuable bulbs of 1637.

We now have a pattern in the evolution of prices of newly developed, fashionable tulip bulbs. The first bulbs, unique or in small supply, carry high prices. With time, the price declines rapidly either because of rapid reproduction of the new variety or because of the increasing introduction of new varieties. Anyone

Table 10.2
Guilder Prices of Tulip Bulbs, 1707, 1722, and 1739

Bulb	1707	1722	1739	Annual % Depreciation	
				1707–22	1722–39
1. Triomphe d'Europe	6.75	0.3	0.2		
2. Premier Noble	409.		1.0	19*	
3. Aigle Noir	110.	0.75	0.3	33	
4. Roi de Fleurs	251.	10.0	0.1	22	27
5. Diamant	71.	2.5	2.0	22	
6. Superintendent		100.	0.12		40
7. Keyzer Kazel de VI		40.	0.5		26
8. Goude Zon, bontlof		15.	10.0		2
9. Roy de Mouritaine		15.	2.0		12
10. Triomphe Royal		10.	1.0		14

Sources: Krelage (1946) and Bradley (1728).
* 1707–1739.

who acquired a rare bulb would have understood this standard pattern of anticipated capital depreciation, at least by the eighteenth century.

To apply this pattern to the post-collapse period, I treat as rare all eighteenth-century bulbs selling for at least 100 guilders (Premier Noble, Aigle Noir, Roi de Fleurs, and Superintendent. For example, Roi de Fleurs would be counted as rare when its price was fl. 251 in 1707. By 1722, its price was fl. 10, so it would no longer be considered rare. The price declined between 1707 and 1722 by 96 percent, and the average annual decline was 21.5 percent. This 21.5 percent annual decline was averaged with similarly computed declines for other rare bulbs to produce an overall average.

Prices for these bulbs declined at an average annual percentage rate of 28.5 percent. From table 9.1, the three costly bulbs of February 1637 (English Admiral, Admirael van der Eyck, and General Rotgans) had an average annual price decline of 32 percent from the peak of the speculation through 1642. Using the eighteenth-century price depreciation rate as a benchmark also followed by expensive bulbs after the mania, we can infer that any price collapse for rare bulbs in February 1637 could not have exceeded 16 percent of peak prices. Thus, the crash of February 1637 for rare bulbs was not of extraordinary magnitude and did not greatly affect the normal time series pattern of rare bulb prices.

Eighteenth-Century Hyacinth Prices

As further evidence of this standard pattern in bulb prices, I now turn to the market for hyacinths. Krelage supplies prices of hyacinths during the eighteenth and nineteenth centuries. Hyacinths replaced tulips at the start of the eighteenth century as the fashionable flower, and once again a large effort arose to innovate beautiful varieties. A speculation similar to that for tulips occurred from 1734 to 1739, leading to the production of reprints of G&W as a warning against unconstrained financial contracting. Table 10.3 indicates the magnitude of the price declines for a few of the more expensive bulbs during the hyacinthmania. The price decline to as low as 10 percent of 1735 prices in some cases was of similar magnitude to the 1637 crash for common tulip bulbs.

Krelage provides long price series for many hyacinths after their introduction. In table 10.3, I have mainly selected the price patterns for bulbs carrying particularly high prices at the time of introduction. Note that the pattern is similar to that for prized tulips in the seventeenth and eighteenth century. Within three decades, prices of even the highest priced bulbs usually fell to 1–2 percent of the original price. Both originally highly priced and inexpensive bulbs converged to a price of from 0.5 to 1 guilder. The average annual rate of price depreciation for bulbs valued at more than 100 guilders (8 observations) was 38 percent, somewhat faster than the depreciation rate for tulip bulbs. For bulbs valued at

Table 10.3
Hyacinth Price Patterns (Guilders)

Bulb	1716	1735	1739	1788	1802	1808
1. Coralijn*	100	12.75	2	0.6	—	—
2. L'Admirable	100	—	1	1.	—	—
3. Starrekroon	200	—	1	0.3	—	0.3
4. Vredenrijck	—	80	16	1.5	—	—
5. Koning Sesostris	—	100	8	1.	1	—
6. Staaten Generaal	—	210	20	1.5	2	—
7. Robijn	—	12	4	1	1	0.5
8. Struijsvogel	—	161	20	—	—	—
9. Miroir	—	141	10	—	—	—

Bulb	1788	1802	1815	1830	1845	1875
10. Comte de la Coste	200	50	1	0.75	0.5	0.15
11. Henri Quatre	50	30	1	3	5	1
12. Van Doeveren	50	—	1	2	1.2	0.75
13. Flos Niger	60	20	10	—	0.25 (1860)	
14. Rex rubrorum	3	1.5	0.3	1	0.35	0.24

Source: Krelage, 645–655.
*Krelage (645) notes that the Coralijn bulb originally sold for 1000 guilders, though he does not include a year.

between 10 and 80 guilders, the annual price depreciation averaged 20 percent.

Modern Bulb Prices

In modern times, new flower bulb varieties can also be highly valuable. Typically, however, new varieties are reproduced in mass by the bulb's developer and marketed at relatively low prices only when a large quantity of bulbs has been produced. Hence, prices for prototype bulbs are usually unavailable. In the few cases where a prototype bulb does change hands, transaction prices are not announced. Information provided in 1987 by officials at the Bloembollencentrum in Haarlem indicates, however, that new varieties of "very special" tulip bulbs sold for about 5000 guilders ($2400 at 1987 exchange rates) per kilo. A small quantity of prototype lily bulbs was sold for 1 million guilders ($480,000 at 1987 exchange rates, $693,000 at 1999 consumer prices), namely, the price of a fine house, a car, a suit of clothes, several tons of wheat, rye, butter, and so forth. Such bulbs can now be reproduced rapidly with tissue growth techniques, so they also would be marketed at relatively low prices.

Was This Episode a "Tulipmania"?

I now examine whether the evidence demands a mania interpretation for the tulip price movements. First, I will dispose of two nagging issues: (1) the absence of descriptions of economic distress in accounts of the period not engaged in antispeculative moralizing, and (2) the claims that the disappearance of renowned bulbs or their extreme price declines over long time periods signal the lunacy of the event. Next, I will isolate the aspect of the speculation for which the evidence provides no compelling explanation, the trading in common bulbs in the period from January 2, 1637, to February 5, 1637.

Where Was the Purported Economic Distress?

Economic histories of the important events and institutions in the Netherlands during this period are detailed, but they hardly mention the tulip speculation. For example, volumes IV and V of *The Cambridge Economic History of Europe* (Rich and Wilson 1975, 1977) do not mention tulips, though the seventeenth-century Dutch are the leading players in these narratives. The period is characterized as a sequence of Dutch commercial and financial triumphs, and economic distress seems not to have materialized in the Netherlands until after the Thirty Years' War ended in 1648. Cooper (1970, 100) does mention the tulip speculation, in one sentence, as an example of the speculative proclivity of the Dutch during this period. Schama (1987) provides a detailed discussion of the events based primarily on Posthumus and Krelage, but he does not depart from the standard interpretation of the mania.

It is not difficult to understand why general economic studies of this period take little notice of "economic distress" arising from the speculation. Because the longer-term price rise occurred only in the rare bulbs, no significant agricultural resources were devoted to expand their cultivation. Krelage (1946, 498) states that all florists in Haarlem maintained their gardens within the city walls until the second half of the eighteenth century. Gardens could be small, since concentrations of large numbers of identical flowers were not valued highly, unlike current fashion.

Because the spectacular price rise in the common bulbs occurred only after the bulbs were in the ground in September 1636, rises in these prices could also have had little effect on the allocation of resources during 1636–1637. To the extent that the speculation had any impact, it would have had an effect only through the distribution of wealth. Little wealth was actually transferred, however; the fees paid out by buyers in the colleges must have evened out over the course of many transactions, though the "wine money" may have indicated a transfer to tavern owners. In addition, after the collapse, only small settlements were required; and of these, few were made. Even the period of uncertainty about the percentage of settlement required could have had little impact; people with little credit to begin with would not have been affected by a cut off of credit until the contracts were straightened out.

Kindleberger, in his new edition of *Manias, Panics, and Crashes* (1996), which dominates the popular mind on the history of bubbles, added a chapter on tulipmania, which had not been in previous editions, to critique my view that the tulipmania was based on fundamentals. He argued that in fact there were signs of continuation of the tulip exuberance because the share prices of the Dutch East India Company doubled between 1630 and 1639, which is three years after the end of the mania. (In nine years, the Dow has quadrupled; but this is not necessarily the sign of irrationality.) But most of this occurred after 1636, rising from 229 in March 1636 to 412 in 1639, nearly a doubling in three years. Of course, the Spanish armies were on the march in 1636, which would have had some effect on East India shares, and by 1639 had been pushed away. When a second Armada that threatened East India trade was destroyed in 1639, things looked rather good again. Trolling for an impact on the real economy from the tulipmania, Kindleberger (1996) then stretches the timing for possible distress from tulipmania into the 1640s: "This perspective undermines one of Garber's points that there could have been no tulipmania because there was no depressed aftermath. In fact the Dutch economy slowed down to a degree in the 1640s before putting on a tremendous spurt from 1650 to 1672" (101).[14]

Bulb Prices Decline Fast: It Is in Their Nature

That the valuable tulips of 1634–1637 later either disappeared or became common is typical of the market dynamics for newly developed bulb varieties, as indicated by price patterns for eighteenth-century tulip and hyacinth bulbs and for modern bulbs. As the bulbs propagate, their prices naturally fall with expanding supply; however, the original bulb owner's bulb stock increases. The discounted value of bulb sales can easily justify extremely high prices for the unique bulb of a new variety. Even the magnitudes of prices for valuable bulbs and their patterns of decline are not out of line with later prices for new varieties of rare bulbs. Single bulbs in the eighteenth century commanded prices as high as 1000 guilders. In this context, the 1000–2000 guilder price of Semper Augustus from 1623 to 1625 or even its 5500 guilder price in 1637 do not appear obviously overvalued.

The Common Bulbs

The only facet of the speculation for which an explanation does not emerge from the evidence is the one-month price surge for *common* bulbs in January 1637, when prices rose up to twentyfold. After February 9, 1637, the first price observation for a common bulb, the Witte Croonen, is available only in 1642.

Claims that prices dropped to less than 10 percent of peak values after the crash must have originated in the officially proposed 3.5 percent contract settlement fee. This did not necessarily reflect the true price decline but simply provided a means of relieving buyers of most of their losses. For example, suppose that a futures contract had established a price of fl. 500 for a bulb but that its settlement price had been fl. 350 after the collapse. This is a substantial loss of fl. 150 that may even have wiped out the buyer if the contract had been taken seriously. Instead, the official proposal would have required a payment on the lost bet of fl. 17.5, but we learn nothing of the post-collapse price of the underlying bulb from the proposed settlement percentage. Because they never cite a specific transaction price (none exist from trades immediately after the crash), authors citing massive price falls must have inferred them from the percentages proposed for contract buyouts, to the extent that they researched the issue at all.

Table 9.1 contains the price data for one-half pound of Witte Croonen bulbs. From February 1637 to 1642, the price depreciated at an annual rate of 76 percent. As an eighteenth-century benchmark rate, I have used 17 percent per year, the average rate of depreciation of all bulbs priced between fl. 10 and fl. 71 in table 10.2. Assuming that after February 1637 Witte Croonen depreciated at this benchmark rate, the price must have collapsed in the crash to 5 percent of its peak price to have attained a 1642 price of fl. 37.5. Thus, Witte Croonen prices rose by about twenty-six times in January 1637 and fell to one-twentieth of their peak value in the first week of February. The eighteenth-century benchmark pattern of price depreciation, however, would have justified a peak price of fl. 84; so the January price is not out of line.

That a precipitous price decline for common bulbs occurred is confirmed by observations on Switsers in chart 5. The peak price for this bulb of 0.17 guilders/aas was attained on February 5, the apparent peak of the market. Data from notarized contracts on February 6 and 9 indicate a sudden decline to 0.11 guilders/aas. This represents a substantial decline from the prices of the first five days of February, but it still substantially exceeds the prices attained on January 23 and is not of the same order of magnitude as the collapse indicated above for Witte Croonen.

Since already valuable bulbs rose by no more than 200–300 percent over a longer duration, the increase and collapse of the relative price of common bulbs is the remarkable feature of this phase of the speculation. Even if detailed, day-to-day information about market events for this period were available, we would be hard pressed to find a market fundamental explanation for these relative price movements. It is clear that the "colleges" generated these prices, although they are echoed in some written contracts. As noted earlier, the college futures markets suffered from a lack of internal control over the nature of contracts, which might have encouraged a speculation of this sort. These markets consisted of a collection of people without equity making ever-increasing numbers of "million dollar bets" with one another with some knowledge that the state would not enforce the contracts. This was no more than a meaningless winter drinking game, played by a plague-ridden population that made use of the vibrant tulip market.

In any case, the price movements of the common bulbs have little to do with the image of the tulipmania that we have inherited from Mackay and his myriad followers, which was all about the astoundingly high prices and bizarre deals for single rare bulbs.

Indeed, discussions on how strange the tulipmania was have until recently centered on the rare bulbs, especially on one often cited, particularly bizarre trade mentioned in Mackay. On this trade, Krelage (1942, 67) states:[15]

In popular articles about the tulipmania the story of a transaction where a whole list of different goods up to a total value of fl 2500 or fl 3000 was paid for a single Viceroy bulb lives on. Even in a foreign book of academic quality it is assumed without further research that this transaction was indeed carried out.

The story however relates to a non-existent transaction. The key can be found in a pamphlet[16] discussing the "wind trade" [i.e., futures speculation] which states "as a wonder for reference of future generations" that in 1636 one could buy "all the following goods for the value of one flower [bulb]

2 lasts of wheat	448 guilders
4 lasts of rye	558
4 well-fed oxen	480
8 well-fed pigs	240
12 well-fed sheep	120
2 oxheads of wine	70
4 tons of 8 guilder beer	32
2 tons butter	192
1000 pounds cheese	120
1 bed with accessories	100
1 stack of clothes	80
1 silver chalice	60
Total	2500 guilders

Add to this a ship to carry all these goods worth fl 500. And one has got fl 3000 for which one cannot buy the best tulip bulb (so the florists say)."

The intent of this statement is to give the reader an idea of the real value of the money spent on a single bulb. Someone, retelling the story, added that this transaction, which he must have considered as actually having taken place, must have involved a Viceroy because one of those bulbs sold, according to other records, for fl 3000. Since that day the story goes around.

Krelage adds that no other records are available of transactions with such different goods and questions whether any seller would want this kind of transaction in a time when food was not scarce.

As an example of yet another author of a "foreign book of academic quality," Kindleberger cannot resist passing on the myth: "Other down-payments consisted of tracts of land, houses, furniture, silver and gold vessels, paintings, a suit and a coat, a coach and dapple gray pair; and for a single Viceroy (rare), valued at Fl. 2500, two lasts (a measure which varies by commodity and locality) of wheat and four of rye, eight pigs, a dozen sheep, two oxheads of wine, four tons of butter, a thousand pounds of cheese, a bed, some clothing, and a silver beaker" Kindleberger (1996, 100–101, crediting Schama and Krelage, 67).

Even a serious historian, Schama (1987, 358), citing the very page from Krelage quoted above, completely ignores the context to emphasize only a bizarre transaction that, according to Krelage, never happened. He even feels free to weave his own fiction around the story: "In all liklihood it was a farmer who paid fl. 2500 for a single Viceroy in the form of two last of wheat and four of rye, four fat oxen, eight pigs, a dozen sheep, two oxheads of wine, four tons of butter, a thousand pounds of cheese, a bed, some clothing, and a silver beaker."

The wonderful tales from the tulipmania are catnip irresistible to those with a taste for crying bubble, even when the stories are so obviously untrue. So perfect are they for didactic use that financial moralizers will always find a ready market for them in a world filled with investors ever fearful of financial Armageddon.

III

The Macro Bubbles

12

A Preliminary View:
The Mississippi and
South Sea Bubbles

The financial dynamics of these speculations assumed remarkably similar forms. Government connivance was at the heart of these schemes. Each involved a company that sought a rapid expansion of its balance sheet through corporate takeovers or acquisition of government debt, financed by successive issues of shares, and with spectacular payoffs to governments. The new waves of shares marketed were offered at successively higher prices. The purchasers of the last wave of shares took the greatest losses when stock prices fell, while the initial buyers generally gained.

Adam Anderson (1787, 123–124) presents a remarkably lucid description of such speculative dynamics in which a sequence of investors buy equal shares in a venture:

A, having one hundred pounds stock in trade, though pretty much in debt, gives it out to be worth three hundred pounds, on account of many privileges and advantages to which he is entitled. B, relying on A's great wisdom and integrity, sues to be admitted partner on those terms, and accordingly buys three

hundred pounds into the partnership. The trade being afterwards given out or discovered to be very improving, C comes
in at five hundred pounds; and afterwards D, at one thousand
one hundred pounds. And the capital is then completed to two
thousand pounds. If the partnership had gone no further than
A and B, then A had got and B had lost one hundred pounds.
If it had stopped at C, then A had got and C had lost two
hundred pounds; and B had been where he was before: but D
also coming in, A gains four hundred pounds, and B two
hundred pounds; and C neither gains nor loses: but D loses six
hundred pounds. Indeed, if A could shew that the said capital
was intrinsically worth four thousand and four hundred
pounds, there would be no harm done to D; and B and C would
have been obliged to him. But if the capital at first was worth
but one hundred pounds, and increased only by subsequent
partnership, it must then be acknowledged that B and C have
been imposed on in their turns, and that unfortunate thought-
less D paid the piper.

Should we, as outside observers, interpret such a sequence of transactions and prices as a bubble? The in-
trinsic value of the venture from the point of view of the
new investors is the crux of the matter.

First, if the original investor falsely claimed that the
venture promised great dividends, though as yet unreal-
ized, he would be committing fraud. The new investors,
however, would be basing their decisions on their per-
ception of market fundamentals. This is a situation of
asymmetric information in which one player has an
incentive to dissemble.

Second, the original investor might use some of
the proceeds from the stock sales to pay high dividends
to the early investors. This would provide concrete

evidence of the great prospects of the venture to new investors. Of course, this twist on the original fraud is known as a Ponzi scheme; but since the "pigeons" are acting on their view of market fundamentals, there is still no bubble.

Third, the great future earnings may actually materialize, thereby satisfying all investors. This result is typical of the early stages of successful companies; and the sequence of stock issues at increasing prices would neither surprise a modern investment banker nor raise the eyebrows of the SEC. In this case, the promised market fundamentals would actually materialize.

Fourth, the projected future earnings, though based on the best available evidence, may fail to materialize. If the evidence of failure appears suddenly, the share price will suffer a precipitous decline, causing late buyers vociferously to regret their purchases. Hindsight will readily identify the blind folly of the investors and, if it is extreme enough, perhaps categorize the event as a bubble. In fact, the traditional definition of a bubble, as in Palgrave (1926, 181), is "any unsound commercial undertaking accompanied by a high degree of speculation." If the undertaking appeared sound at the start, however, and only looks foolish in hindsight, economists should classify this event as being driven by market fundamentals.

Finally, all investors may understand perfectly well that the venture has no chance of paying large dividends but that a sequence of share buyers at ever increasing prices is available. Investors buy in on a gamble that they will not be in the last wave of buyers. The modern economics literature refers to this scenario as a bubble or chain letter. We now consider whether the Mississippi and South Sea episodes can fit only in the last category.

13

John Law and the
Fundamentals of the
Mississippi and
South Sea Bubbles

John Law's Financial System

Both the Mississippi and South Sea Bubbles can best be understood in the context of the monetary theory and system created by John Law.[17] Law is not well known today, but Schumpeter (1954, 295), for example, is unreserved in praising him: "He worked out the economics of his projects with a brilliance and, yes, profundity which places him in the front ranks of monetary theorists of all times."

Law sketched a monetary theory in an environment of unemployed resources. In such an environment, he argued ([1705] 1760, 190–191), an emission of paper currency would expand real commerce permanently, thereby increasing the demand for the new currency sufficiently to preclude pressure on prices. To finance a great economic project, an entrepreneur needed only the power to create claims that served as a means of payment. Once financed, the project would profit sufficiently from the employment of previously wasted resources to justify the public's faith in its liabilities.

Economic policy advocates and their ideas, good or bad, float to the surface only when they provide a convenient pretext for politicians to impose their preferred schemes. Law's idea got its chance in France in 1715. France had been bankrupted by the wars of Louis XIV. In a situation recently repeated by Russia in 1998, France had repudiated part of its internal debt, forced a reduction in interest due on the remainder, and was still in arrears on its debt servicing. High taxes, combined with a tax system full of privileges and exemptions, had seriously depressed economic activity.

The French economic environment was well suited for Law's scheme, and he quickly convinced the Regent to permit him to open a conventional, note-issuing bank in June 1716, the Banque Generale. In August 1717, Law organized the Compagnie d'Occident to take over the monopoly on trade with Louisiana and on trade in Canadian beaver skins. This line of business is the source of the word "Mississippi" in characterizing Law's system.

To finance the company, Law took subscriptions on shares to be paid partly in cash but mostly in government debt. He then converted the government's debt into long-term *rentes*, offering the government an interest-rate reduction.

The idea was to establish a solid "fund of credit," a certain cash inflow that, when capitalized, could be leveraged to undertake the grand commercial schemes that lay at the heart of Law's economic theory. The nature of Law's scheme was that finance of the operation came first; expanded commercial activity would result naturally once the financial structure was in place.

In effect, the French privatized the treasury under Law's plan and had only to wait for the general commercial expansion promised by Law's theory to materialize and to support the market prices of the company's shares.

The Compagnie d'Occident did increase its commercial activity, obtaining the tobacco monopoly in September 1718 and the Senegalese Company for trade with Africa, that is, the slave trade, in November 1718.[18] In January 1719, the Banque General was taken over by the regent and renamed the Banque Royale, with a note issue guaranteed by the crown. Law remained in control of the new bank. In May 1719, he acquired the East India Company and the China Company; and he reorganized the entire conglomerate as the Compagnie des Indes, an organization that monopolized all French trade outside Europe.

On July 25, 1719, the Compagnie purchased the right to mint new coinage for fifty million livres tournois to be delivered in fifteen monthly payments. The *livre tournois* was the unit of account and was officially valued at weights of gold or silver that varied during Law's regime. To finance this expenditure, Law issued 50,000 shares at 1000 livres per share to cover this acquisition, requiring share buyers to hold five previously issued shares. Share prices rose to 1800 livres.

In August 1719, the Compagnie bought the right to collect all French indirect taxes for a payment to the government of 52 million livres per year. The takeover of the administration of the tax system was in line with Law's views that a simplified fiscal regime would benefit commerce and reduce the costs of collection. Law thought that taxes should be broad-based and few, with no exemptions or privileges. He set about reorganizing the personnel of the tax system, because a reduced collection cost would be a source of company profit. In October 1719, he took over the collection of direct taxes. Share prices rose to 3000 livres.

Finally, Law determined to refund most of the national debt through the Compagnie des Indes, an amount with a face value of 1.5 billion livres. The face value of the entire debt was estimated by Harsin (1928) at about two billion livres; the market value of the debt was well below the par value because of previous defaults and arrearages.

To finance the debt acquisition, Law undertook a sequence of three stock sales on September 12, September 28, and October 2, 1719. In each offering, the Compagnie sold 100,000 shares at 5000 livres per share payable in ten equal monthly payments. Payment could be made either at par in *rentes* or in the notes of the Banque Royale. Thus, by August 1720, enough would have been raised to acquire the face value of the debt.

Of the 540,000 shares then outstanding of the Compagnie des Indes, the King held 100,000 shares and therefore was counted a powerful backer of the scheme. In addition, the Compagnie itself held 100,000 shares that it could sell. Researchers of the Mississippi and South Sea episodes treat the quantity of own shares held by the companies as significant. There was a limitation on authorized share issues, so shares held by the company provided a source of cash to fuel company finance activities as prices rose.

Acquiring the debt would create a huge "fund of credit," a steady income flow from the government, which could be used as equity against any potential commercial venture of the Compagnie. Simultaneously, the Compagnie would reduce the interest paid by the state to 3 percent per year. After these operations, share prices rose to 10,000 livres in October 1719.

The shares outstanding would then have had a market value of 5.4 billion livres, somewhat less than four times the face value of the rentes that were the most tangible assets of the Compagnie. For perspective, Law estimated the national wealth of France at 30 billion livres.

Law attained maximum power in January 1720 when he was made France's Controller General and Superintendent General of Finance. As an official, he now controlled all government finance and expenditure and the money creation of the Banque Royale. Simultaneously, he was the chief executive officer of a private firm that controlled France's overseas trade and the development of its colonies, collected France's taxes, minted its coins, and held the bulk of France's national debt. The king was a principal shareholder of the firm. It must have been obvious to all that the Compagnie would find few government or financial obstacles to its undertaking any commercial scheme that it chose. Surely no economist has since had a better set of conditions for testing a major economic theory than that possessed by Law.

Figure 14.1 illustrates the Mississippi bubble. The phase of price increase is associated with the expanding activity of the Compagnie at this time.

In the end, however, the commercial scheme chosen was to print money. Starting with the July 1719 stock issue, the Banque Royale had increased its note issue to facilitate the stock sales. Each government authorization of a share expansion simultaneously authorized a note emission.

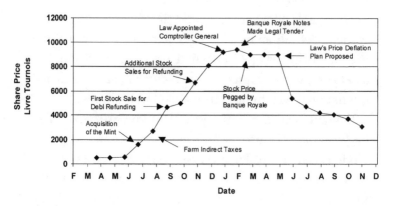

Figure 14.1
Daily South Sea Share Prices, 1720

For example, with only 159 million livres in notes previously authorized, the Banque received authorization to emit 240 million livres on July 25, 1719. A further 240 million livre expansion was associated with the September and October share sales. Additional note issues of 360 million and 200 million livres occurred on December 29, 1719, and February 6, 1720, respectively, without new share issues. For comparison, Harsin (1928) estimates the total specie stock of France at about 1.2 billion livres. The money creation was used to provide loans to buyers of the shares. This reduced the number of floating shares, replacing them with bank notes. Because Law regarded shares as a superior form of currency, this did not increase the "money supply" in his view.

The ultimate control on such wealth surges through rising valuation is the attempt by shareholders to convert their capital gains into current goods or gold. The surge of goods supply needed to meet this demand did not currently exist and in Law's theory would be realized in amounts adequate to match demand stemming from high share values only after the fruition of the projects. Even if there was a chance for his operations to pay off, the short-term finance of his operations through the monetization of the shares was to be the fatal financial flaw of the scheme.

By the end of January 1720, share prices had begun to fall below 10,000 livres because of increasing attempts to convert capital gains into a gold form. The falling price of shares threatened Law's ability to use his "fund of credit" to begin a commercial expansion.

In January 1720, Law began to act against the use of specie in payments by prohibiting payments above 100 livres in metallic money. On February 22, 1720, the Compagnie took over direct control of the management of the Banque Royale; and the Banque Royale's notes were made legal tender for payments above 100 livres. Simultaneously, the King sold his 100,000 shares back to the Compagnie at 9000 livres per share. Of this amount, three hundred million livres would be deposited in the King's accounts in the Banque immediately with the rest to be paid over ten years. The Compagnie then ceased supporting the price of its shares with banknotes, precipitating a sharp price decline. Thus, the most powerful insider bailed out near the peak of the speculation.

Law criticized unsophisticated shareholders trying to convert shares to the concrete form of gold because there was not enough gold in the kingdom to satisfy such an attempt. Law stated that the shares had high value only if they were regarded as a capital investment, to be bought and sold infrequently, held by people content to receive their yields as a flow of dividends that he claimed was somewhat higher than the prevailing interest rate.[19]

On March 5, 1720, share prices were pegged at 9000 livres: the Banque Royale now intervened directly to exchange its notes for Compagnie stock. Effectively converting shares into banknotes with a denomination of 9000 livres, this policy was a realization of Law's theory that a commercial enterprise could finance itself with emissions of circulating debt. Until its termination on May 21, 1720, the pegging scheme generated legal tender note expansions of 300 million, 390 million, 438 million, and 362 million livres on March 25, April 5, April 19, and May 1, respectively, to absorb sales by shareholders. The Banque's legal tender note circulation doubled in about one month.

This also was a doubling in the money stock, because the circulating metallic stock of money had by then disappeared. In an effort to drive out metallic currency and to maintain the facade of note convertibility, Law had simultaneously imposed a series of drastic devaluations of specie in terms of livre tournois. As a result of this dramatic monetary expansion, the average monthly inflation rate from August 1719 through September 1720 was 4 percent, with a peak of 23 percent in January 1720. The index of commodity prices increased from 116.1 in July 1719 to 203.7 in September 1720 (Hamilton 1936–37). Figure 14.2 depicts how the sequence of bank note issues drove the currency supply and the price level.

Deciding that the price of shares had been fixed at too high a level, Law proposed a drastic deflation on May 21, 1720.[20] Share prices would be reduced from 9000 to 5000 livres in seven stages, ending on December 1. Banque notes would be reduced in value to 50 percent of their face value—that is, he would force a restructuring on

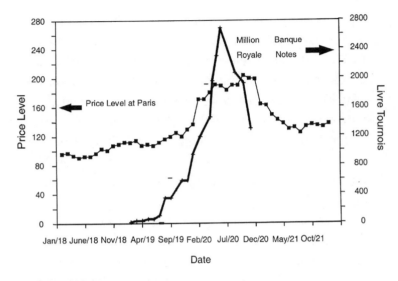

Figure 14.2
Mississippi Bubble Money and Price Data

holders of the Banque Royale's liabilities. Under this plan by December, only 2.3 billion livres in paper asset values (1.3 billion in Banque notes and 1 billion in stock) would remain. This reduction was actually accomplished by various other means. Law's plan simply to write down the value of the Banque notes in terms of livre tournois was abandoned when he was thrown from office at the end of May 1720. He was, however, quickly reappointed and presided over the deflation.

By October 1720, only 1.2 billion livres of notes remained in circulation (of a peak of 2.7 billion) and 1.2 billion livres of specie reappeared. Specie was rapidly revalued to the definition that it had at the start of 1720.

By December 1720, the price level had fallen to 164.2. Thus, the period starting in February 1720 represents an initial period of share price pegging by the Banque—that is, the monetization of shares—followed by the purposeful monetary and share price deflation undertaken by Law.

The price of the Compagnie's shares fell to 2000 livres in September 1720 and to 1000 livres by December. Law's enemies were now in a position to impose policies hostile to the Compagnie, notably a confiscation of two-thirds of the shares outstanding. The share price fell to 500 livres by September 1721, approximately its value in May 1719.

15   A Rehash of Mississippi Market Fundamentals

Should economists sum up the increasing stock prices of the Compagnie des Indes only as the "Mississippi bubble"? After all, behind the price rise lies Law's program to revitalize the French economy through financial innovation and fiscal reform. Law's theory was plausible and even has many modern manifestations, and he was an effective propagandist. Investors also could readily observe Law's astounding rise to power. At each stage, as the implementation of the economic experiment became ever more likely, they had to factor the possibility of success into the share prices of the Compagnie des Indes.

The downward slide of share prices is even easier to understand, given the radical shifts in monetary policy and the intimate connection of Compagnie shares to Banque Royale note emissions. The final fall to original share values was driven by Law's fall from power and the accession of his enemies, who aimed to dismantle the Compagnie.

That Law's promised expansion never materialized does not imply that a bubble occurred in the modern sense of the word. After all, this was not the last time that a convincing economic idea would fracture in practice. One respectable group of modern economists or another have described Keynesian economics, supply side economics, monetarism, fixed exchange-rate regimes, floating exchange-rate regimes, and the belief in rational expectations in asset markets as disastrously flawed schemes. Indeed, elements of the first three were primary components in Law's scheme.

Only after the experiment had been run could investors have known that the idea was flawed. That they referred to the ensuing collapse and their after-the-fact foolishness as a bubble should not confuse economists' interpretation of the event. According to the modern definition in economics, the event is easily explainable on the basis of market fundamentals. For a finance operation to be successful always requires a certain degree of sustained confidence from investors. Finance serves as the spearhead of corporate rationalization. In any leveraged buyout or corporate acquisition, high securities prices come first and are followed only gradually by expanded revenues. If investors suddenly lose confidence, they may turn a potentially profitable project into a bankruptcy if it is financed with short-term funding.

Law's scheme was more audacious than the normal Wall Street operation in that he was attempting a corporate takeover of France. But Law's principle was also that finance came first; the financial operation and the expansion of circulating credit was the driving force for economic expansion. From a modern perspective, this idea is not flawed. It is the centerpiece of most money and macroeconomics textbooks produced in the last two generations and the lingua franca of economic policymakers concerned with the problem of underemployed economies. Indeed, recent pressure on the Bank of Japan to monetize long-term government bonds is a scheme that Law would have found familiar.

Law's mistake was that he recognized the accelerating price inflation as inconsistent with the prediction of his theory. His launching of the deflation was similar to any modern restructuring effort to eliminate an excessive debt overhang. Because of the programmed share price fall and the ensuing declines forced by his removal from power, his experiment is tarred with the perjorative "bubble." When modern economic policymakers' reach exceeds their grasp, they simply accommodate the ensuing tenfold price inflation and get the Nobel prize.

Law's Shadow: The South Sea Bubble

Following Law's scheme to refinance the French debt, the South Sea Company launched a similar plan to acquire British government debt in January 1720.[21] The financial operations of the British scheme, however, were much simpler than those of Law: the South Sea Company was not involved in large-scale takeovers of commercial companies or of government functions such as the mint, the collection of taxes, or the creation of legal tender paper money.

The British debt in 1720 amounted to approximately £50 million of face value. Of this, £18.3 million was held by the three largest corporations: £3.4 million by the Bank of England, £3.2 million by the East India Company, and £11.7 million by the South Sea Company. Redeemable government bonds held privately amounted to £16.5 million; these could be called by the government on short notice. About £15 million of the debt was in the form of irredeemable annuities: long annuities of between seventy-two and eighty-seven years and short annuities of twenty-two years in maturity.[22]

The Refunding Agreement

In 1720, the assets of the South Sea Company consisted of monopoly rights on British trade with the South Seas—that is, the Spanish colonies of America—and its holdings of government debt. These were treaty rights to trade on a small scale and especially to export slaves. It was well known that British trade with Spanish America was effectively blocked by the Spanish and in any case unprofitable, so only the holdings of government debt are important to the economic story. After competitive bidding between the South Sea Company and the Bank of England, the bill permitting the South Sea Company to refund the debt had its first passage in Parliament on March 21, 1720. To acquire this right, the company agreed to pay the government up to £7.5 million if it managed to acquire the £31 million of debt held in noncorporate hands.

To finance the debt acquisition, the Company was permitted to expand the number of its shares, each of which had a par value of £100. For each £100 per year of the long and short annuities acquired, the company could increase the par value of its shares outstanding by £2000 and by £1400, respectively. For each £100 par value of redeemables acquired, it could increase its stock issue by £100.

Quantities of shares were designated in terms of total par value issued. Most research on the episode has continued this convention and has emphasized the difference between the market and par value of shares. The company was free to set the exchange rate between shares and debt. It valued the shares exchanged at well above the par value, leaving it an excess of authorized shares that it was free to market. Scott (1911) labeled these surplus shares the company's "profits" from the conversion. The curious view that a company's holdings of its own shares represents an asset has been replicated in recent examinations of the South Sea Company; for instance, Dickson (1967, 160) lists the company's holdings of its own stock among its assets.

The interest to be paid by the government on the debt acquired by the company was 5 percent per year until 1727 and 4 percent per year thereafter. This would imply a substantial reduction in the annual debt servicing costs of the government.

The Purchase of Parliament

Conditional on the passage of the refunding act, the South Sea Company paid bribes to leading members of Parliament and favorites of the king totaling £1.3 million (Scott 1911, 315). Moreover, in the sequence of stock subscriptions through August 1720, numerous members of Parliament and of the government participated; and most received large cash loans from the company on their shares. For example, 128 members of Parliament acquired shares in the first cash subscriptions for shares, 190 in the second subscription, 352 in the third subscription, and 76 in the fourth subscription. The total par value of shares acquired by them was £1.1 million. For peers, the participation was 58 in the first subscription, 73 in the second subscription, 119 in the third subscription, and 56 in the fourth subscription. The total par value for peers was £548,000. Prior to the refunding operation, the par value of South Sea shares outstanding was £11.7 million; and this was increased to £22.8 million by the end of the speculation. Thus, people in powerful positions in Parliament took 17 percent of the additional shares created. In addition, as Dickson (1967, 108–109) explains, 132 members of Parliament received £1.1 million and 64 peers received £686,000 in loans against shares. Members of the government acquired £75,000 of shares at par value in these subscriptions.

While these bribes add a sinister appearance to the episode, they were not themselves a signal of impending fraud. At the time, bribery was not an unusual practice for a company seeking favors from a Parliament well positioned to block any profitable venture unless its members received their cut.

Indeed, that Parliament and the government supported the refunding so enthusiastically must have served as a signal that official cooperation in South Sea's ventures had been purchased. To the extent that members of Parliament held shares, they would have no interest in thwarting any commercial projects that the company might propose in the future. Given Law's influential theories of commercial expansion, the equity in the South Sea Company could then have been leveraged to undertake those commercial projects that would drive the economy to a higher employment equilibrium. The income generated, accruing to the company without hindrance of Parliament, could in theory then have justified the initial value of the equity—provided that there were such projects.

17 South Sea Finance Operations

Figure 17.1 depicts the movement of South Sea share prices during the speculation. Starting at about £120 per £100 par value share in January 1720, prices moved upward as the refunding proposal was negotiated. With the passage of the refunding act on March 21, prices jumped from about £200 to £300.

To finance the contracted bribes and to make loans to shareholders, the Company offered two subscriptions of shares for cash on April 14 and April 29. In the first subscription, 22,500 shares were issued at a price of £300 per share; one-fifth of the price was required immediately in cash with the remainder due in eight bimonthly installments. In the second, 15,000 shares were subscribed at a price of £400; one-tenth was required immediately in cash, with the remainder due in nine payments at three- or four-month intervals. From these issues, the company immediately realized about £2 million to pay its bribe commitments.

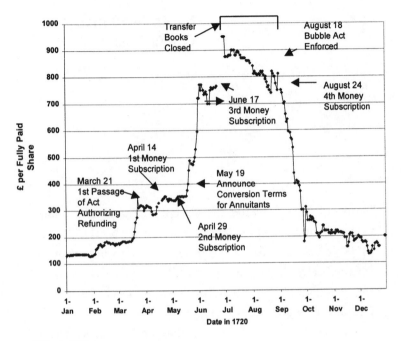

Figure 17.1
Daily South Sea Share Prices, 1720. Data courtesy of Larry Neal.

The first debt conversion aimed at convincing the holders of the irredeemable annuities to agree to an exchange for South Sea shares. Subscriptions began on April 28. The company announced its conversion terms on May 19, allowing holders of the debt one week to accept or reject the conversion terms, which depended on the type of annuity. As an example, the holders of £100 long annuities were offered £700 par value of stock (7 shares) and £575 in bonds and cash. At the time of the offer, South Sea shares were selling for about £400, so the value of the offer was about £3375 for a long annuity. Scott (1911, 311) estimates the market value of the annuity at about £1600 prior to the conversion attempt. Since annuity holders would not lose unless share prices fell below £146, the offer was highly attractive.

All government creditors who had subscribed prior to the announcement assented to the company's terms. According to Dickson (1967, 130–132), the company therefore absorbed about 64 percent of the long annuities and 52 percent of the short annuities outstanding in this subscription. As it became clear that the company would succeed in accumulating most of the outstanding debt, share prices rose rapidly to £700.

To permit it sufficient cash to engage in market price manipulation and to make loans to its shareholders, the company undertook a third cash subscription on June 17, 1720, in which it sold a par value of £5 million (50,000 shares) for a market price of £1000 per share. Purchasers had to pay one-tenth down in cash (£5 million), with the remainder to be paid in nine semi-annual payments. Share prices immediately jumped from £745 to £950. The final cash subscription occurred on August 24. The company sold 12,500 shares with a par value of £1.25 million at a price of £1000 per share. One-fifth was required immediately in cash, with four additional payments at nine-month intervals. From June 24 to August 22, the transfer books of the company were closed in preparation for a dividend payment, so the market prices depicted in figure 17.1 for this period were future prices.[23]

Finally, the company offered two additional subscriptions for government bonds; terms for subscribing the remaining irredeemables and the redeemables were announced on August 4 and August 12, respectively. Of the outstanding £16.5 million in redeemables, £14.4 million were exchanged for 18,900 shares of stock. At market prices of £800 per share, this amounted to a price of £105 per £100 bond. Redeemables were callable by the government, so this price, although seemingly low in comparison to the irredeemables, was generally acceptable. The remaining irredeemables were to be exchanged for varying amounts of stock and cash. By means of all the debt conversions, the South Sea Company acquired 80 percent of the public's holdings of the irredeemables and 85 percent of the redeemables.

The Price Collapse

South Sea share prices collapsed from about £775 on August 31 to about £290 on October 1, 1720. Shares outstanding or to be issued to the public after subscribers were entered on company registers numbered 212,012. Thus, the market value of all shares on August 31 was £164 million and about £103 million of that total evaporated in one month, an amount exceeding twice the value of the original, burdensome government debt.

Researchers of the episode like Dickson (1967, 148–152), Scott (1911, 324–328), and Neal (1988) are vague about the reason for the speed and magnitude of the decline, though they generally attribute it to the appearance of a liquidity crisis. The South Sea speculation had triggered a simultaneous upsurge in the prices of other existing companies along with the creation of numerous "bubble companies." The emergence of these companies, many of which were fraudulent, generated most of the amusing anecdotes that have been transmitted to us about this speculation. Many of the companies born in the 1720 speculation were quite sound, however, notably the Royal Assurance Company and the London Assurance Company. The channeling of capital into these companies alarmed the directors of the South Sea Company, who, having paid a high price to buy the Parliament, did not wish to see potential South Sea profits dissipated by the entry of unauthorized commercial corporations. Consequently, Parliament passed the Bubble Act in June 1720 to ban the formation of unauthorized corporations or the extension of existing corporate charters into new, unauthorized ventures.

When the Bubble Act was enforced against some of the company's competitors on August 18, 1720, immediate downward pressure was placed on the price of shares of the affected companies. Because the shares were mostly held on margin, general selling hit the shares of all companies, including South Sea shares, in a scramble for liquidity. Simultaneously, there was an international scramble for liquidity with the final collapse of Law's Compagnie des Indes in September 1720 and of a Dutch speculation. Liquidity may have been drained from

English markets by these international events. Neal and Schubert (1985) provide evidence on large-scale capital movements during this period.

With the collapse of share prices, the South Sea Company faced the hostility of its shareholders who had participated in its debt and cash subscriptions. Parliament quickly turned against the company, eventually forcing it to sell off part of its debt holdings to the Bank of England. Parliament eventually stripped the directors of the company and several government officials of their wealth (£2 million) and directed the payment of the proceeds to the South Sea Company. Adjustments were also made to redistribute shares among the different waves of subscribers, so that losses to later subscribers were reduced. Finally, Parliament forgave payment of the £7.1 million that the company had contracted on receipt of the conversion privilege.

18 Fundamentals of the South Sea Company

At the beginning of September 1720, the market value of South Sea shares was £164 million. The visible asset supporting this price was a flow of revenue from the company's claim against the government of £1.9 million per year until 1727 and £1.5 million thereafter. At a 4 percent long-term discount rate, this asset had a value of about £40 million. Against this, the company had agreed to pay £7.1 million for the conversion privilege and owed £6 million in bonds and bills for a net asset value of £26.1 million. In addition, the company's cash receivables were £11 million due on loans to stockholders and £70 million eventually due from cash subscribers. Thus, share values exceeded asset values by more than £60 million. Given the dubious value of the company's cash claims, share values exceeded tangible net assets by five times or more.

What intangible assets could have justified this value of the company? Again, the answer lies in Law's prediction of a commercial expansion associated with the accumulation of a fund of credit. The company succeeded in gathering the fund and obviously had the support of Parliament in its ventures. On this basis, Scott (1911, 313–314) believed that a price of £400 was not excessive.

It may be added too that the great need of commerce in the first quarter of the eighteenth century was a sufficiency of capital, and so it is scarcely possible to estimate adequately, under the different conditions of the present time, the many promising outlets there were then for the remunerative employment of capital. In fact capital, organized in one single unit, might be utilized in many directions, where no single fraction of the same capital could find its way, and therefore some premium on South Sea stock was justified and maintainable. . . . Thus, it will be seen that the investor, who in 1720 bought stock at 300 or even 400, may have been unduly optimistic, but there was at least a possibility that his confidence would be rewarded in the future.

The experiment was terminated with the liquidity crisis and the withdrawal of parliamentary support while it was still in its finance stage. In retrospect, anyone projecting commercial returns high enough to justify the higher prices of South Sea shares was probably too optimistic. Nevertheless, the episode is readily understandable as a case of speculators' working on the basis of the best economic analysis available and pushing prices along by their changing view of market fundamentals.

19   Conclusion

The jargon of economics and finance contains numerous colorful expressions to denote a market-determined asset price at odds with any reasonable economic explanation. Such terms as *tulipmania, bubble, chain letter, Ponzi scheme, panic, crash,* and *financial crisis* immediately evoke images of frenzied and irrational speculative activity. Lately, the same terms, or modern versions of them—*herding, irrational exhuberance, contagion,* and *self-generating equilibrium*—have been used by media, academics, and policymakers to paint the crises of 1997, 1998, and 1999.

These words are always used to argue the irrationality of financial markets in particularly volatile periods. Many of these terms have emerged from specific speculative episodes, which have been sufficiently frequent and important that they underpin a strong current belief that key capital markets generate irrational and inefficient pricing and allocational outcomes.

The proponents of such arguments can hardly ever resist the invocation of three famous bubbles—the Dutch tulipmania, the Mississippi Bubble, and the South Sea Bubble. That such obvious craziness happened in the past is taken as the only necessary explanation for modern events that are otherwise hard to explain with their favorite economic theories.

Before we relegate a speculative event to the fundamentally inexplicable or bubble category driven by crowd psychology, however, we should exhaust the reasonable economic explanations. Such explanations are often not easily generated due to the inherent complexity of economic phenomena, but bubble explanations are often clutched as a first and not a last resort. Indeed, "bubble" characterizations should be a last resort because they are non-explanations of events, merely a name that we attach to a financial phenomenon that we have not invested sufficiently in understanding. Invoking crowd psychology—which is always ill defined and unmeasured—turns our explanation to tautology in a self-deluding attempt to say something more than a confession of confusion.

Fascinated by the brilliance of grand speculative events, observers of financial markets have huddled in the bubble interpretation and have neglected an examination of potential market fundamentals. The ready availability of a banal explanation of the tulipmania, compared to its dominant position in the speculative pantheon of economics, is stark evidence of how bubble and mania characterizations have served to divert us from understanding those outlying events highest in informational content. The bubble interpretation has relegated the far more important Mississippi and South Sea episodes to a description of pathologies of group psychology. Yet these events were a vast macroeconomic and financial experiment, imposed on a scale and with a degree of control by their main theoretical architects that did not occur again until the war economies of this century. True, the experiment failed, either because its theoretical basis was fundamentally flawed or because its managers lacked the complex financial skills required to undertake the day-to-day tactics necessary for its consummation. Nevertheless, investors *had* to take positions on its potential success. It is curious that students of finance and economists alike have accepted the failure of the experiments as proof that the investors were foolishly and irrationally wrong.

An observation that the tulipmania and the Mississippi and South Sea Bubbles predispose us to advance bubble theories of asset pricing provided the point of departure of this study. If small strata of particular episodes underpin the belief that bubbles may exist, it is desirable to undertake a detailed study of these events, most of which have not been examined from the perspective of market fundamental theories of asset pricing, to assure that other reasonable explanations have not been overlooked.

In the end, one can take one's pick: market fundamental explanations of events or bubble and crowd psychology theories. It is my view that bubble theories are the easy way out—they are simply names that we attach to that part of asset price movements that we cannot easily explain. As tautological explanations, they can never be refuted. The goal here is to find explanations with some measure of economic and refutable content.

Appendix 1   The Tulipmania in the Popular and Economics Literature

Chroniclers of the tulip speculation, and modern writers who cite it, take for granted that it was a mania, selecting and organizing the evidence to emphasize the irrationality of the market outcome.

In the twentieth century, a strong intellectual influence on participants and observers of the financial markets has been exerted by Mackay's version of the tulipmania, although he devoted only seven pages of text to it. Bernard Baruch wrote an introduction to Mackay's book, whose reprinting he had encouraged, emphasizing the importance of crowd psychology in all economic movements. Dreman (1977), who also stresses psychological forces in asset price determination, uses the tulipmania as a prototype of market mania. Relating the same anecdotes as Mackay, Dreman employs the tulipmania as a constant metaphor in discussions of succeeding major speculative collapses. He states (52):

If, for example, my neighbor tried to sell me a tulip bulb for $5,000, I'd simply laugh at him.... The tulip craze, like the manias we shall see shortly, created its own reality as it went along. It is ludicrous to pay as much for a flower as one pays for a house. . . .[24]

Whenever large and rapid fluctuations of asset prices occur, the popular media recall the tulipmania. For example, when gold prices jumped in 1979, a *Wall Street Journal* (Sept. 26, 1979) article stated, "The ongoing frenzy in the gold market may be only an illusion of crowds, a modern repetition of the tulip-bulb craze or the South Sea Bubble." The October 19, 1987, stock market crash brought forth similar comparisons from the *Wall Street Journal* (Dec. 11, 1987); and *The Economist* (Oct. 24, 1987) explained the event as follows:

The crash suffered by the world's stockmarkets has provided a beginning and middle for a new chapter updating Charles Mackay's 1841 book "Extraordinary Popular Delusions and the Madness of Crowds" which chronicled Dutch tulip bulbs, the South Sea bubble. . . . It was the madness of crowds that sent the bull market ever upward. . . . It is mob psychology that has now sent investors so rapidly for the exits. (P. 75)

Malkiel (1985) cites Mackay extensively in his chapter "The Madness of Crowds," including the anecdote about the sailor and the claim that the collapse led to a pro-longed depression in Holland. In reference to other speculative episodes, he asks:

Why do such speculative crazes seem so isolated from the lessons of history? I have no apt answer to offer, but I am convinced that Bernard Baruch was correct in suggesting that a study of these events can help equip investors for survival. The consistent losers in the market, from my personal experience, are those who are unable to resist being swept up in some kind of tulip-bulb craze. (Pp. 44–45)

Galbraith (1993) simply repeats Mackay's story about the tulipmania without any effort at serious research to include succeeding developments in knowledge on the topic. Krugman (1995) could not resist invoking the tulipmania in discussing emerging market capital flows.

On a more serious note, the pre–1950s academic literature written by major professional economists contains little direct reference to the tulipmania. *Palgrave's Dictionary of Political Economy* (1926, 182) includes a paragraph on tulips in its section on bubbles, citing Mackay. In earlier editions of his cubist study of manias, Kindleberger (1978) catalogued a long sequence of financial panics and manias and provided a descriptive pathology of their dynamics; but he did not include the tulipmania among those episodes examined in detail because "manias such as . . . the tulip mania of 1634 are too isolated and lack the characteristic monetary features that come with the spread of banking" (6). In his article on "bubbles" in *The New Palgrave Dictionary of Economics* (Eatwell, Milgate, and Newman 1987), however, Kindleberger includes the tulipmania as one of the two most famous manias. In the most recent edition of his book on manias, Kindleberger (1996) added a chapter critiquing earlier papers that I had written on tulipmania.

The tulipmania made its first appearance in serious economics journals with the development of capital theory in the 1950s and the discovery of the potential existence of multiple, dynamically unstable asset price paths. Samuelson (1957, 1967) presents the tulipmania metaphor and associates it with "the purely financial dream world of indefinite group self-fulfillment" (1967, 230). Samuelson (1957) uses "tulipmania" interchangeably with "Ponzi scheme," "chain letter," and "bubble."

Students of Samuelson, in a flurry of research activity concerning the "Hahn problem," employ the tulipmania as an empirical motivation. Shell and Stiglitz (1967) state, "The instability of the Hahn model is suggestive of the economic forces operating during 'speculative booms' like the Tulip Bulb mania." Burmeister (1980, 264–286) summarizes these models.

The advent of the "sunspot" literature generated a revival of references to tulips as a motivation for the line of research. For example, Azariadis (1981, 380) argues that "the evidence on the influence of subjective factors is ample and dates back several centuries; the Dutch 'tulip mania,' the South Sea bubble in England, and the collapse of the Mississippi Company in France are three well-documented cases of speculative price movements that historians consider unwarranted by 'objective' conditions." More recently, Azariadis and Guesnerie (1986) state, "And the reading of economic historians may suggest that these factors (sunspots) have some pertinence for the explanation of phenomena like the Dutch tulipmania in the seventeenth century and the Great Depression in our own" (725).

Under the topic "tulipmania" in *The New Palgrave Dictionary of Economics* (Eatwell, Milgate, and Newman 1987), Guillermo Calvo does not refer to the seventeenth-century Dutch speculative episode at all. Rather, he defines tulipmania as a situation in which asset prices do not behave in ways explainable by economic fundamentals. He develops examples of rational bubbles, both of the explosive and "sunspot" varieties. In the finance literature, the emergence of empirical anomalies has also generated references to tulipmania as bubble and fad explanations have regained respectability. In his presidential address to the American Finance Association, van Horne (1985), embraces the possibility of bubbles and manias and, as an example, refers explicitly to the tulipmania, where a "single bulb sold for many years' salary."

Appendix 2   The Seventeenth-Century Tulip Price Data

Table A2.1 contains price data for various tulips. For each type of bulb, the observations are ordered by date; they include the price paid, the weight in aas of the bulb, the price per aas, and the data source. I have gathered the data from different sources of uneven reliability.

Some sources are marked with numbers to indicate the numbering of notarized contracts reported by Posthumus in *Economisch-Historisch Jaarboek* (1927, 1934). Because these were carefully drawn contracts sworn before notaries, they are the most reliable data, representing serious transactions that did not occur in the colleges. Furthermore, many are dated before the peak of the speculation in January–February 1637. Presumably, the contracts drawn from June to September were for spot delivery. The delivery dates for the winter contracts are unclear. A few contract prices reported in Krelage (1946) are labeled as "Krelage–46-p482."

Next in order of reliability are the bulbs labeled "Children," which I have taken from *Economisch-Historisch*

Jaarboek (1927). These bulbs are taken from a price list labeled "List of some tulips sold to the highest bidder on February 5, 1637, in the city of Alkmaar. These tulips were sold to the benefit of the children of Mr. Wouter Bartelmiesz at a total amount of Fl. 68,553." A facsimile of this list is also reproduced in Krelage (1946, 488). Again, the delivery date and terms of payment are not clear from the available information. Also, the February 5 date seems at odds with the collapse date, which G&W claim occurred on February 3. However, as recorded auction prices, the list represents some actual transactions.

Lower in order of reliability are the numerous prices reported in G&W. G&W is in the form of a long and moralistic dialogue between Gaergoedt (Greedy Goods) and Waermondt (True Mouth) about the nature of the markets and the price dynamics during the speculation. The third dialogue, "Prijsen der Bloemen," presents a list of about 250 bulb transactions, including prices and weights, but it does not report the dates of the sales. Fortunately, since a great deal of overlap appears between the G&W prices and the "Children" prices, the author of G&W must have had access to the "Children" list in constructing the G&W list. Thus, I used the February 5 date of the "Children list to date the reported prices in the G&W list, including those G&W flowers not reported in the "Children" list. Moreover, finding many of the G&W flowers listed among verifiable transactions generates some confidence that the G&W author did not simply make up the prices reported in the third dialogue.

In discussing the rapidity of price movement during the speculation, G&W present the prices of twenty bulbs observed at two different times in the speculation, claiming the earlier prices were taken from four to six weeks prior to the later prices for each bulb. However, they do not indicate the dates on which the later transactions occurred. Fortunately, most of the later transactions for these bulbs are among the bulbs in the "Children" list or in the extensive G&W list described above. Since these bulbs are the only "time series" reported in G&W, it is important to include them. Thus, I have presumed that the later transaction for each bulb occurred on February 5, 1637, and that the earlier transaction occurred on January 2, 1637, five weeks earlier. This explains why so many January 2–February 5 pairs appear in the list in table A2.1.

Finally, the list contains several transactions listed in Munting (1672, 1696) and in Krelage (1942) that I could not find among the above sources. Unfortunately, Krelage reports the price per aas involved in particular transactions and not the price and weight of the transacted bulb.

Table A2.1
Basic Tulip Price Data

Date	Tulip	Price	Weight	Price/Aas	Source	Place
01-Jun-36	Admirael Liefkens	6.6	1	6.6000	18	Haarlem
05-Feb-37	Admirael Liefkens			11.8000	Krelage, 49	
05-Feb-37	Admirael Liefkens	4,400	400	11.0000	G&W	
05-Feb-37	Admirael Liefkens	1,015	59	17.2034	Children	Alkmaer
02-Jan-37	Admirael de Man	15	130	0.1154	G&W	
02-Jan-37	Admirael de Man	90	1,000	0.0900	G&W	
05-Feb-37	Admirael de Man	250	175	1.4286	G&W	
05-Feb-37	Admirael de Man	800	1,000	0.8000	G&W	
05-Feb-37	Admirael de Man	175	130	1.3462	G&W	
05-Feb-37	Admirael van Enchuysen	5,400	215	25.1163	G&W	
05-Feb-37	Admirael van Enchuysen			28.0000	Krelage, 49	
05-Feb-37	Admirael van Enchuysen	900	8	112.5000	G&W	
05-Feb-37	Admirael van Hoorn	230	1,000	0.2300	G&W	
05-Feb-37	Admirael van Hoorn	200	440	0.4545	G&W	
01-Dec-34	Admirael van der Eyck	80	80	1.0000	7	Haarlem
01-Dec-34	Admirael van der Eyck	66	20	3.3000	7	Haarlem

Date	Variety					
27-Jul-36	Admirael van der Eyck	2.5	1	2.5000	17	Haarlem
05-Feb-37	Admirael van der Eyck			4.5000	Krelage, 49	Alkmaer
05-Feb-37	Admirael van der Eyck	1,620	446	3.6323	Children	Alkmaer
05-Feb-37	Admirael van der Eyck	1,045	214	4.8832	Children	Alkmaer
05-Feb-37	Admirael van der Eyck	710	92	7.7174	Children	Alkmaer
01-Dec-36	Bleyenburch (Laeten)	350	4 tulips		57	Amsterdam
28-Dec-36	Bleyenburch (Laeten)	120	104	1.1538	65	Amsterdam
05-Feb-37	Blijenburger (Vroege)			3.5000	Krelage, 49	
05-Feb-37	Blijenburger (Vroege)	1,300	443	2.9345	Children	Alkmaer
05-Feb-37	Blijenburger (Vroege)	900	171	5.2632	Children	Alkmaer
05-Feb-37	Bruyne Purper	2,025	320	6.3281	Children	Alkmaer
05-Feb-37	Bruyne Purper			10.3000	Krelage, 49	
05-Feb-37	Bruyne Purper	1,100	50	22.0000	G&W	
05-Feb-37	Bruyne Purper	1,300	60	21.6667	G&W	
10-Jul-12	Caers op de Candelaer	24			3	Haarlem
02-Jan-37	Centen	40	1,000	0.0400	G&W	
15-Jan-37	Centen	72	530	0.1358	van Damme, 106	
22-Jan-37	Centen	380	3,000	0.1267	32	Amsterdam
05-Feb-37	Centen	400	1,000	0.4000	G&W	
05-Feb-37	Centen	4,300	10,240	0.4199	G&W	

Table A2.1 (continued)

Date	Tulip	Price	Weight	Price/Aas	Source	Place
02-Jan-37	Coorenaerts	60	1,000	0.0600	G&W	
22-Jan-37	Coorenaerts	220	1,000	0.2200	32	Amsterdam
05-Feb-37	Coorenaerts	550	1,000	0.5500	G&W	
05-Feb-37	Coorenaerts	4,800	10,240	0.4688	G&W	
10-Jun-36	English Admiral	3	1	3.0000	13	
05-Feb-37	English Admiral	700	25	28.0000	G&W	
05-Feb-37	Fama	605	130	4.6538	Children	Alkmaer
05-Feb-37	Fama	700	158	4.4304	Children	Alkmaer
05-Feb-37	Fama	440	104	4.2308	Children	Alkmaer
02-Jan-37	Generalissimo	95	10	9.5000	G&W	
05-Feb-37	Generalissimo	900	10	90.0000	G&W	
02-Jan-37	Gheele Croonen	24	10,240	0.0023	G&W	
05-Feb-37	Gheele Croonen	1,200	10,240	0.1172	G&W	
08-Dec-36	Gheele ende Roote van Leyden	260	578	0.4498	Krelage, 73	
02-Jan-37	Gheele ende Roote van Leyden	46	515	0.0893	G&W	
02-Jan-37	Gheele ende Roote van Leyden	100	1,000	0.1000	G&W	
05-Feb-37	Gheele ende Roote van Leyden	700	1,000	0.7000	G&W	

Date	Name					
05-Feb-37	Gheele ende Roote van Leyden	140	400	0.3500	G&W	
05-Feb-37	Gheele ende Roote van Leyden	550	515	1.0680	G&W	
05-Feb-37	Gheele ende Roote van Leyden			0.5800	Krelage, 49	
05-Feb-37	Gheele ende Roote van Leyden	235	240	0.9792	G&W	
12-Nov-36	Ghemarm. de Goyer	70	357	0.1961	Krelage, 73	
04-Feb-37	Ghemarm. de Goyer	36	1 bulb		van Damme, 21	
05-Feb-37	Ghemarm. de Goyer	250	1,000	0.2500	G&W	
05-Feb-37	Gouda			7.5000	Krelage, 49	
01-Dec-34	Gouda	45	30	1.5000	7&Krelage, 49	Haarlem
01-Dec-35	Gouda	2.1	1	2.1000	24	Haarlem
29-Aug-36	Gouda	3.75	1	3.7500	20	Haarlem
25-Nov-36	Gouda	446	66	6.7576	30	Haarlem
09-Dec-36	Gouda	600	400	1.5000	35	Haarlem
12-Dec-36	Gouda	520	48	10.8333	Laubach, 87	
02-Jan-37	Gouda	20	4	5.0000	G&W	
29-Jan-37	Gouda	100	7	14.2857	33	Haarlem
05-Feb-37	Gouda	3,600	1,000	3.6000	Munting & G&W	
05-Feb-37	Gouda	1,500	244	6.1475	Children	Alkmaer
05-Feb-37	Gouda	1,330	187	7.1123	Children	Alkmaer
05-Feb-37	Gouda	1,165	160	7.2813	Children	Alkmaer

Table A2.1 (continued)

Date	Tulip	Price	Weight	Price/Aas	Source	Place
05-Feb-37	Gouda	1,165	156	7.4679	Children	Alkmaer
05-Feb-37	Gouda	1,015	125	8.1200	Children	Alkmaer
05-Feb-37	Gouda	765	82	9.3293	Children	Alkmaer
05-Feb-37	Gouda	635	63	10.0794	Children	Alkmaer
05-Feb-37	Gouda	225	4	56.2500	G&W&30	Haarlem
29-Sep-36	Groote Geplumiceerde	140	2,000	0.0700	28	Amsterdam
12-Jan-37	Groote Geplumiceerde	300	2,000	0.1500	G&W	
05-Feb-37	Groote Geplumiceerde	300	400	0.7500	71	Haarlem
05-Feb-37	Groote Geplumiceerde	280	1,000	0.2800	Children	Alkmaer
05-Feb-37	Groote Gepulmiceerde	300	1,000	0.3000	G&W	
15-Jan-37	Jan Gerritsz	230	288	0.7986	van Damme, 104	
05-Feb-37	Jan Gerritsz	734	1,000	0.7340	G&W	
05-Feb-37	Jan Gerritsz	210	263	0.7985	Children	Alkmaer
05-Feb-37	Jan Gerritsz (Swijmende)	210	925	0.2270	Children	Alkmaer
05-Feb-37	Jan Gerritsz (Swijmende)	51	80	0.6375	Children	Alkmaer
05-Feb-37	Julius Caesar	1,300	187	6.9519	G&W	
18-Dec-35	Latour	27	16	1.6875	9	Haarlem

Date	Name					City
05-Feb-37	Latour	390	450	0.8667	G&W	Haarlem
16-Jan-37	Le Grand	90	122	0.7377	Krel-46-p482	Amsterdam
22-Jan-37	Le Grand	21	185	0.1135	32	Haarlem
24-Jan-37	Le Grand	480	1,000	0.4800	31	Alkmaer
05-Feb-37	Le Grand	500	350	1.4286	Children	
05-Feb-37	Le Grand	780	1,000	0.7800	G&W	
24-Jan-37	Macx	12	400	0.0300	31	Haarlem
03-Feb-37	Macx	400	2,000	0.2000	75	Amsterdam
05-Feb-37	Macx	300	1,000	0.3000	Children	Alkmaer
05-Feb-37	Macx	300	1,000	0.3000	Children	Alkmaer
05-Feb-37	Macx	390	700	0.5571	G&W	
06-Jan-37	Nieuwburger	125	425	0.2941	65	Amsterdam
05-Feb-37	Nieuwburger	500	1,000	0.5000	G&W	
05-Feb-37	Nieuwburger	390	495	0.7879	G&W	
05-Feb-37	Nieuwburger	235	500	0.4700	Children	Alkmaer
05-Feb-37	Nieuwburger	430	1,000	0.4300	Children	Alkmaer
05-Feb-37	Nieuwburger	180	495	0.3636	G&W	
01-Dec-36	Oudenaerden	600	10,240	0.0586	57	Amsterdam
02-Jan-37	Oudenaerden	70	1,000	0.0700	G&W	

Table A2.1 (continued)

Date	Tulip	Price	Weight	Price/Aas	Source	Place
22-Jan-37	Oudenaerden	1,430	5,120	0.2793	32	Amsterdam
30-Jan-37	Oudenaerden	2,200	4,864	0.4523	Krel-46-p482	Haarlem
05-Feb-37	Oudenaerden	600	1,000	0.6000	G&W	
05-Feb-37	Oudenaerden	370	450	0.8222	Children	Alkmaer
05-Feb-37	Oudenaerden	530	1,000	0.5300	Children	Alkmaer
05-Feb-37	Oudenaerden	510	1,000	0.5100	G&W	
05-Feb-37	Oudenaerden	5,700	10,240	0.5566	G&W	
17-May-33	Parragon Schilder	50	1 Bulb		34-2	Amsterdam
05-Feb-37	Parragon Schilder	1,615	106	15.2358	G&W	
16-Dec-36	Petter	172	360	0.4778	van Damme, 103	
05-Feb-37	Petter	900	800	1.1250	G&W	
05-Feb-37	Petter	730	1,000	0.7300	Children	Alkmaer
05-Feb-37	Petter	705	1,000	0.7050	Children	Alkmaer
05-Feb-37	Petter	730	1,000	0.7300	G&W	
05-Feb-37	Rotgans	805	1,000	0.8050	Children	Alkmaer
05-Feb-37	Rotgans (Violette Gevlamde)	725	1,000	0.7250	Children	Alkmaer
05-Feb-37	Rotgans (Violette Gevlamde)	375	500	0.7500	Children	Alkmaer

18-Dec-35	Saeyblom van Coningh	30	7.5	4.0000	9	Haarlem
05-Feb-37	Saeyblom van Coningh	320	220	1.4545	G&W	
05-Feb-37	Saeyblom, beste	1,000	1,000	1.0000	G&W	
05-Feb-37	Schapesteyn	235	95	2.4737	Children	Alkmaer
05-Feb-37	Schapesteyn	375	246	1.5244	Children	Alkmaer
02-Jan-37	Scipio	800	1,000	0.8000	G&W	
12-Jan-37	Scipio	1,500	1,000	1.5000	28	Amsterdam
05-Feb-37	Scipio	100	10	10.0000	G&W	
05-Feb-37	Scipio	400	82	4.8780	Children	Alkmaer
05-Feb-37	Scipio	2,250	1,000	2.2500	G&W	
01-Jul-23	Semper Augustus	1,000	1 bulb		Krelage, 32	
01-Jul-24	Semper Augustus	1,200	1 bulb		Posthumus	
01-Jul-25	Semper Augustus	2,000	1 bulb		Krelage, 33	
05-Feb-37	Semper Augustus	5,500	200	27.5000	Munting	
02-Jan-37	Switsers	60	10,240	0.0059	G&W	
15-Jan-37	Switsers	120	9,728	0.0123	34	Haarlem
22-Jan-37	Switsers	280	10,240	0.0273	32	Amsterdam
23-Jan-37	Switsers	385	10,240	0.0376	Krelage, 51	
01-Feb-37	Switsers	1,400	9,728	0.1439	75	Amsterdam

Table A2.1 (continued)

Date	Tulip	Price	Weight	Price/Aas	Source	Place
03-Feb-37	Switsers	6,000	40,960	0.1465	38	Amsterdam
05-Feb-37	Switsers	1,800	10,240	0.1758	G&W	
06-Feb-37	Switsers	1,100	10,240	0.1074	34-6	Amsterdam
06-Feb-37	Switsers	1,060	10,240	0.1035	34-5	Amsterdam
09-Feb-37	Switsers	1,100	10,240	0.1074	40	Haarlem
02-Jan-37	Viceroy	3,000	1,000	3.0000	G&W	
05-Feb-37	Viceroy	4,203	685	6.1358	Children	Alkmaer
05-Feb-37	Viceroy	3,000	410	7.3171	Children	Alkmaer
05-Feb-37	Viceroy	2,700	295	9.1525	G&W	
05-Feb-37	Viceroy	6,700	1,000	6.7000	G&W	
10-Jul-12	Vlaems	450	38,912	0.0116	4	Haarlem
02-Jan-37	Witte Croonen	128	10,240	0.0125	G&W	
05-Feb-37	Witte Croonen	300	1,000	0.3000	G&W	
05-Feb-37	Witte Croonen	3,600	10,240	0.3516	G&W	
05-Feb-37	Witte Croonen			0.2700	Krelage, 49	
05-Feb-37	Zomerschoon	1,010	368	2.7446	G&W	

Notes

1. The discussion of political and economic history is based on Rich and Wilson, *The Cambridge Economic History of Europe*, vols. 4 and 5 (Rich and Wilson 1975, 1977); Braudel (1979), vol. 3; Attman (1983); and Cooper, *The New Cambridge Modern History of Europe*, vol. IV (1970).

2. See Attman (1983, 35). The guilder was the unit of account. It was denoted by the sign fl. (florin) and was divided into 20 stuivers. The stuiver was further subdivided into 16 pennings. The guilder was a bimetallic unit, equivalent to 10.75 grams of fine silver from 1610–1614, 10.28 grams from 1620–1659, and 9.74 grams thereafter. See Posthumus (1964, cxv) and Rich and Wilson (1977, 458). Its gold content was 0.867 grams of fine gold in 1612, 0.856 grams in 1622, 0.77 in 1638, and 0.73 in 1645. This was a devaluation of gold content of 16%. See Posthumus (1964, cxix). Prices of foodstuffs, metals, and fibers did not display significant secular movements from 1600 through 1750; so given the orders of magnitude of bulb price changes that we will observe, we can take the price level as approximately constant in interpreting nominal prices during this 150-year period.

3. See Penso de la Vega ([1688] 1957) for a description of the variety of securities and the sophistication of market manipulation on the Amsterdam exchange.

4. Beckmann wrote originally in German at the end of the eighteenth century; only the fourth English edition (1846) of his book was available to me.

5. For a list of these pamphlets, see the references in Krelage (1942, 1946).

6. These were published in *the Weekblad voor Bloembollencultur* and are reprinted in Van Damme (1976).

7. The discussion in this section is based on Schama (1987, 323–371), and on the translation of Penso de la Vega (1688, xii–xix).

8. See Prinzing (1916) on the epidemics of the Thirty Years' War. See also Cooper (1970, 76).

9. See Mather (1961, 44).

10. See Doorenbos (1954, 1–11).

11. See Mather (1961, 100–101).

12. See Posthumus (1929, 442).

13. Gheele Croonen and Witte Croonen apparently were not broken tulips, though they were multicolored. However, it is not clear whether all the other "pound good" tulips were broken.

14. In his discussion on economic distress in the tulipmania, Malkiel asks, "And what of those who had sold out early in the game? In the end, they too were engulfed by the tulip craze. For the final chapter of this bizarre story is that the shock generated by the boom and collapse was followed by a prolonged depression in Holland. No one was spared" (1996, 38). Unfortunately, there was no depression in Holland. Malkiel prefers to propagate the myth handed down by Mackay to seriously researching the topic.

15. I thank Guido Imbens and Klaas Baks for this translation.

16. Krelage cites "Clare ontdeckingh der ghener, die haer tegenwoordigh laten noemen Floristen" (Hoorn: Zacharias Cornelisz, 1636) as the source.

17. This section is intended as a brief outline of the vast Mississippi scheme. For a recent fascinating view of the scheme and its implementation, see Antoin Murphy's excellent *John Law* and also his biography of Richard Cantillon. Larry Neal (1990) provides a general description of the development of the financial markets in England, the Netherlands, and France in the eighteenth century, along with an analysis of the South Sea and Mississippi bubbles.

18. This outline of Law's experiment is based on descriptions in Harsin (1928), Faure (1977), and Murphy (1986).

19. See Harsin's (1928, 180) citation of Law's *Deuxieme Lettre sur le nouveau system des finances.*

20. Murphy (1997, 235) argues that Law was pushed into the share price fixing phase during a temporary loss of control.

21. I have taken the factual information in this section primarily from Scott (1911), Carswell (1960), and Dickson (1967).

22. Neal (1988) discusses the nature of these annuities.

23. Neal (1988) argues that the peak price was £950 on July 1. Scott (1911) indicates a peak price of £1050, but this apparently includes the announced stock dividend of 10 percent. Following Neal, I have used the peak price of £950.

24. Dreman clearly neglected to inquire about current bulb prices in Haarlem before he wrote.

References

Anderson, A. 1787. *An Historical and Chronological Deduction of the Origin of Commerce*, vol. 3. London: J. Walter.

Attman, A. 1983. *Dutch Enterprise in the World Bullion Trade*. Goteborg: Almqvist and Wicksell.

Azariadis, C. 1981. "Self-Fulfilling Prophecies." *Journal of Economic Theory* 25:380–396.

Azariadis, C., and R. Guesnerie. 1986. "Sunspots and Cycles." *Review of Economic Studies* 53 (Oct.):725–737.

Beckmann, J. 1846. *History of Inventions, Discoveries, and Origins*, vol. 1, 4th ed. London: Harry G. Bohn.

Bradley, R. 1728. *Dictionarium Botanicum: Or, a Botanical Dictionary for the Use of the Curious in Husbandry and Gardening*. London.

Braudel, F. 1979. *The Perspective of the World*. Vol. 3, *Civilization & Capitalism, 15th–18th Century*. New York: Harper and Row.

Burmeister, E. 1980. *Capital Theory and Dynamics*. Cambridge: Cambridge University Press.

Carswell, J. 1960. *The South Sea Bubble*. London: Cresset Press.

"Clare ontdeckingh der ghener, die haer tegenwoordigh laten noemen Floristen." 1636. Hoorn: Zacharias Cornelisz.

Cooper, P. 1970. *New Cambridge Modern History*. Vol. IV, *The Decline of Spain and the Thirty Years' War*. Cambridge: Cambridge University Press.

D'Ardene, J. 1760. *Traité des Tulipes*. Avignon: Chambeau.

de Vries, J. 1976. *The Economy of Europe in an Age of Crisis, 1600–1750*. Cambridge: Cambridge University Press.

Dickson, P. G. M. 1967. *The Financial Revolution in England: A Study in the Development of Public Credit*. London: Macmillan.

Doorenbos, J., "Notes on the History of Bulb Breeding in the Netherlands." *Euphytica* 3, no. 1 (February 1954):1–11.

Dreman, D. 1977. *Psychology and the Stock Market*. New York: Anacom.

Eatwell, J., M. Milgate, and P. Newman, eds. 1987. *The New Palgrave Dictionary of Economics*. Dictionary oillan.

Faure, E. 1977. *La Banqueroute de Law*. Paris.

Galbraith, J. K. 1993. *A Short History of Financial Euphoria*. New York: Viking.

Garber, P. 1989. "Tulipmania." *Journal of Political Economy* (April): 535–560.

———. 1990a. "Famous First Bubbles." *Journal of Economic Perspectives* (May): 35–54.

———. 1990b. "Who Put the Mania in Tulipmania?" In E. White, ed., *Crashes and Panics: The Lessons from History*. Homewood, IL: Dow-Jones Irwin.

Hamilton, E. 1936–37. "Prices and Wages at Paris under John Law's System." *Quarterly Journal of Economics* 51:42–70.

Harsin, P. 1928. *Les Doctrines Monetarires et Financieres en France*. Paris: Librairie Felix Alcan.

Hartman, H., and D. Kester. 1983. *Plant Propagation*. Englewood Cliffs, NJ: Prentice-Hall.

International Monetary Fund. 1998. *World Economic Outlook and International Capital Markets, Interim Assessment*. Washington, DC: IMF.

Kindleberger, C. 1978. *Manias, Panics, and Crashes*. New York: Basic Books.

Kindleberger, C. P. 1996. *Manias, Panics, and Crashes: A History of Financial Crises*, 3d ed. New York: Wiley.

Krelage, E. H. 1942. *Bloemenspeculatie in Nederland*. Amsterdam: P. N. van Kampen & Zoon.

———. 1946. *Drie Eeuwen Bloembollenexport*, Vol 2. s'Gravenhage.

Krugman, P. 1995. "Dutch Tulips and Emerging Markets." *Foreign Affairs* 74:28–44.

La Chesnee Monstereul. 1654. *Le Floriste François*. Caen: Mangeant.

Law, J. [1705] 1760. *Money and Trade Considered: With a Proposal for Supplying the Nation with Money*. Glasgow: Foulis.

"Liste van Eenige Tulpaen . . ." [1637] 1927. In *Economisch-Historisch Jaarboek*, vol. XII, 96–99. Reprint, Haarlem: Adriaen Roman.

Mackay, C. [1841] 1852. *Extraordinary Popular Delusions and the Madness of Crowds*, vol. 1, 2d ed. London: Office of the National Illustrated Library.

Malkiel, B. 1985. "The Madness of Crowds." In *A Random Walk Down Wall Street*, 4th ed. New York: Norton.

Malkiel, B. G. 1996. *A Random Walk Down Wall Street*. New York: Norton.

Mather, J. 1961. *Commercial Production of Tulips and Daffodils*. London: WH&L.

Munting, A. 1672. *Waare Oeffening der Planten*. Amsterdam.

———. 1696. *Naauwkeurige Beschryving der Aardgewassen*. Leyden.

Murphy, A. E. 1986. *Richard Cantillon, Entrepreneur and Economist*. Oxford: Clarendon Press.

——. 1997. *John Law: Economic Theorist and Policy-Maker.* Oxford: Clarendon Press.

Neal, L. 1988. "How the South Sea Bubble Was Blown Up and Burst: A New Look at Old Data." University of Illinois Working Paper, August.

——. 1990. *The Rise of Financial Capitalism.* Oxford: Cambridge University Press.

Neal, L., and E. Schubert. 1985. "The First Rational Bubbles: A New Look at the Mississippi and South Sea Schemes." BEBR Working Paper 1188, University of Illinois, Urbana-Champaign, September.

Palgrave, R. H. 1926. *Dictionary of Political Economy.* London: MacMillan.

Penso de la Vega, J. [1688, Amsterdam] 1957. *Confusion de Confusiones*, English trans. Boston: Baker Library.

Posthumus, N. W. 1926, 1927, 1934. "Die Speculatie in Tulpen in de Jaren 1636–37." *Economisch-Historisch Jaarboek.*

——. 1929. "The Tulip Mania in Holland in the Years 1636 and 1637." *Journal of Economic and Business History* 1 (May).

——. 1964. *Inquiry into the History of Prices in Holland.* Leiden: E. J. Brill.

Prinzing, F. 1916. *Epidemics Resulting from Wars.* Oxford: Clarendon Press.

"Register den de Prijsen der Bloemen . . . Derde Samenspraeck." [1637] 1926. In *Economisch-Historisch Jaarboek*, vol. XII. Reprint, Haarlem: Adriaen Roman.

Rich, E. E., and C. H. Wilson, eds. 1975. *The Cambridge Economic History of Europe.* Vol. IV, *The Economy of Expanding Europe in the Sixteenth and Seventeenth Centuries.* London: Cambridge University Press.

——. 1977. *The Cambridge Economic History of Europe.* Vol. V, *The Economic Organization of Early Modern Europe.* London: Cambridge University Press.

The Royal General Bulbgrowers Society. 1969. *Classified List and International Register of Tulip Names.* Haarlem.

"Samenspraeck Tusschen Waermondt ende Gaergoedt: Flora." [1637] 1926. In *Economisch-Historisch Jaarboek*, vol. XII. Reprint, Haarlem: Adriaen Roman.

Samuelson, P. A. 1957. "Intertemporal Price Equilibrium: A Prologue to the Theory of Speculation." *Weltwirtschaftliches Archiv* 79, no. 2:181–219; reprinted in J. Stiglitz, ed., *The Collected Scientific Papers of Paul A. Samuelson*, vol. 2. Cambridge: The MIT Press, 1966.

———. 1967. "Indeterminacy of Development in a Heterogeneous-Capital Model with Constant Saving Propensity." In K. Shell, ed.,*Essays on the Theory of Optimal Economic Growth*. Cambridge: The MIT Press.

Schama, S. 1987. *The Embarrassment of Riches*. New York: Alfred Knopf.

Schumpeter, J. 1954. *History of Economic Analysis*. New York: Oxford University Press.

Scott, W. 1911. *The Constitution and Finance of English, Scottish, and Irish Joint Stock Companies to 1720*, vol. 2. Cambridge: Cambridge University Press.

Shell, K., and J. Stiglitz. 1967. "The Allocation of Investment in a Dynamic Economy." *Quarterly Journal of Economics* 81, no. 4 (November):592–609.

Smith, K. 1937. *Textbook of Plant Virus Diseases*. London: J&A Churchill.

Solms-Laubach, H. Graf. 1899. *Weizen und Tulpe und deren Geschichte*. Leipzig: Felix.

"Tweede Samenspraeck Tusschen Waermondt ende Gaergoedt." [1637] 1926. In *Economisch-Historisch Jaarboek*, vol. XII. Reprint, Haarlem: Adriaen Roman.

van Damme, A. 1976. *Aanteekeningen Betreffende de Geschiedenis der Bloembollen, Haarlem 1899–1903*. Leiden: Boerhaave Press.

van Horne, J. 1985. "Of Financial Innovations and Excesses." *Journal of Finance* 40, no. 3 (July):621–631.

van Slogteren, E. 1960. "Broken Tulips." In *The Daffodil and Tulip Yearbook*, 25–31. London: Royal Horticultural Society.

Index